Holt MUSIC

Eunice Boardman Meske
Professor of Music and Education
University of Wisconsin—Madison
Madison, Wisconsin

Barbara Andress
Professor of Music Education
Arizona State University
Tempe, Arizona

Mary P. Pautz
Assistant Professor of Music
  Education
University of Wisconsin—Milwaukee
Milwaukee, Wisconsin

Fred Willman
Professor of Music and Education
University of Missouri—St. Louis
St. Louis, Missouri

Holt, Rinehart and Winston, Publishers
New York, Toronto, Mexico City, London, Sydney, Tokyo

Special Consultants

Nancy Archer
Forest Park Elementary School
Fort Wayne, Indiana

Joan Z. Fyfe
Jericho Public Schools
Jericho, New York

Jeanne Hook
Albuquerque Public Schools
Albuquerque, New Mexico

Danette Littleton
University of Tennessee at Chattanooga
Chattanooga, Tennessee

Barbara Reeder Lundquist
University of Washington
Seattle, Washington

Ollie McFarland
Detroit Public Schools
Detroit, Michigan

Faith Norwood
Harnett County School District
North Carolina

Linda K. Price
Richardson Independent School District
Richardson, Texas

Dawn L. Reynolds
District of Columbia Public Schools
Washington, D.C.

Morris Stevens
A.N. McCallum High School
Austin, Texas

Jack Noble White
Texas Boys Choir
Fort Worth, Texas

ISBN 0-03-005268-8

9012 041 98765

Acknowledgments for previously copyrighted materials
and credits for photographs and art start on page 174.

Table of Contents

Unit 1

Music To Explore

Make up music

Clap

chant

Read music

Sing

Move

play instruments

Whistle While You Work

Words and Music by
Larry Morey and Frank Churchill

Just whistle while you work.

(whistle)

Put on that **grin** and start right in to **whistle** loud and long.

Just hum a merry tune.

(hum)

Just do your best, then take a **rest**

and sing your-self a song.

LISTENING

Wooden Flute

from *Mala Suite*

by Witold Lutoslawski

The high sounds in this music
sound very much like our whistling.

7

You'll Sing a Song and I'll Sing a Song

Words and Music by Ella Jenkins

This picture will help you learn the song.

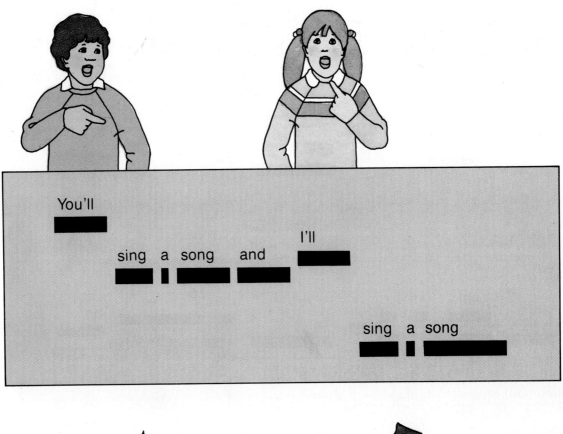

You'll ▮ sing a song and I'll ▮

sing a song ▮

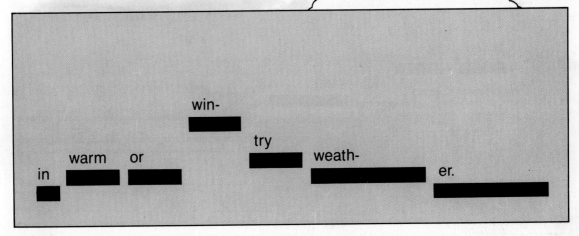

in ▮ warm ▮ or ▮ win- ▮ try ▮ weath- ▮ er. ▮

I Live in a City

Words and Music by Malvina Reynolds

Refrain

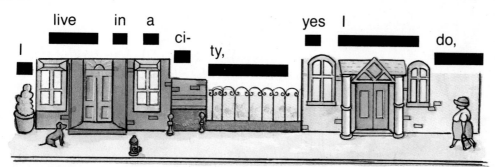

I live in a ci-ty, yes I do,

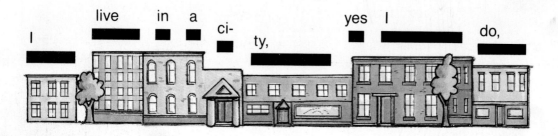

I live in a ci-ty, yes I do,

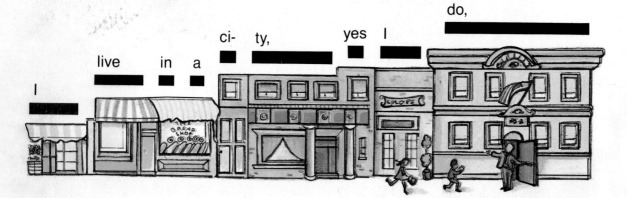

I live in a ci-ty, yes I do,

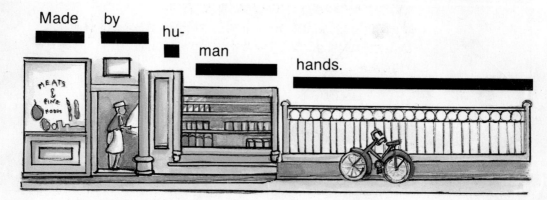

Made by hu-man hands.

Verse

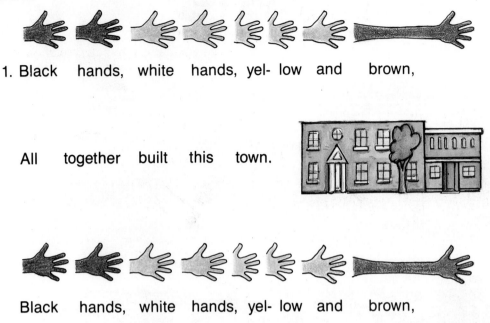

1. Black   hands,   white   hands,   yel- low   and   brown,

All   together   built   this   town.

Black   hands,   white   hands,   yel- low   and   brown,

All together   make   the   wheels   go 'round.

2. Brown hands, yellow hands, white and black,
   Mined the coal and built the stack.
   Brown hands, yellow hands, white and black,
   Built the engine and laid the track.
   Refrain

3. Black hands, brown hands, yellow and white,
   Built the buildings tall and bright.
   Black hands, brown hands, yellow and white,
   Filled them all with shining light.
   Refrain

4. Black hands, white hands, brown and tan,
   Milled the flour and cleaned the pan.
   Black hands, white hands, brown and tan,
   The working woman and the working man.
   Refrain

The Tired Caterpillar

Words Anonymous

Music by Haydn Morgan

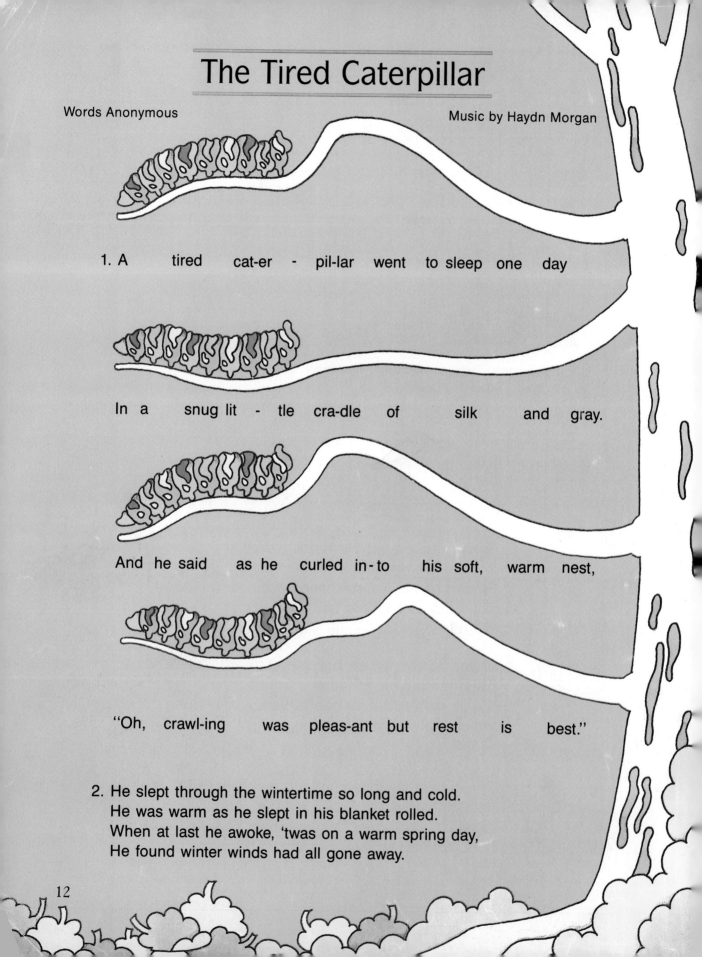

1. A   tired   cat-er - pil-lar   went   to sleep   one   day

In a   snug lit - tle   cra-dle   of   silk   and   gray.

And he said   as he   curled in - to   his soft,   warm   nest,

"Oh,   crawl-ing   was   pleas-ant but   rest   is   best."

2. He slept through the wintertime so long and cold.
   He was warm as he slept in his blanket rolled.
   When at last he awoke, 'twas on a warm spring day,
   He found winter winds had all gone away.

12

3. When he wa - kened he found that he had gold - en wings

And no more would he crawl on top of sticks and things.

"While the earth's ve-ry nice—," said the but - ter - fly,

"The sky still is best when we learn to fly."

The Grand Old Duke of York

(soft)

(loud)

(loud)

He marched them up to the top of the hill And marched them down again.

The grand old Duke of York,
His men were half asleep.

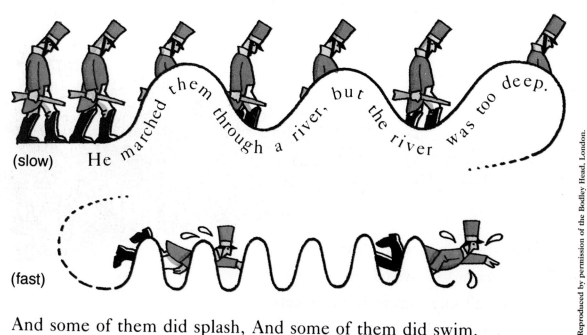

(slow) He marched them through a river, but the river was too deep.

(fast)

And some of them did splash, And some of them did swim.

14

The grand old Duke of York,
He found himself alone.
He sat right down on the top of a drum
And there did weep and moan.

His men they all were lost,
His horse away had run.

The grand old Duke of York,
He heard a bugle sound.

He jumped right up and looked about,
His heart began to pound.

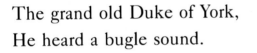

He saw them in rows of five,
He saw them in rows of ten,
And they all lined up in front of him
Till he had ten thousand men.

The Mysterious Cat

Poem by Vachel Lindsay
Paintings by Paul Klee

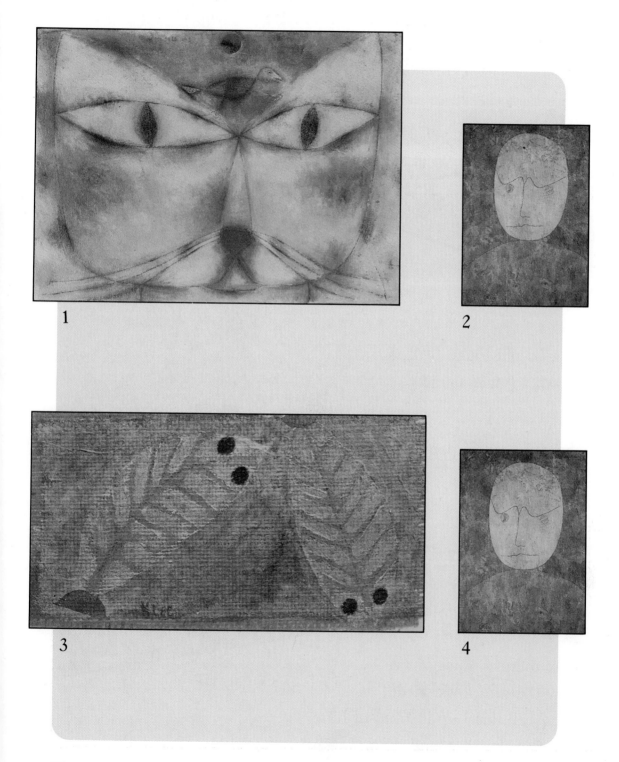

1

2

3

4

5

6

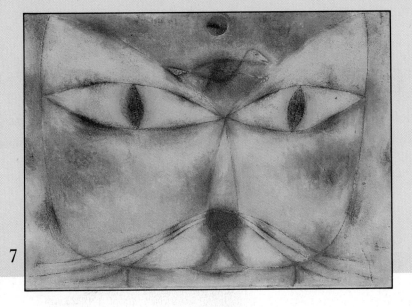

7

La Chatte

from *L'Enfant et les sortilèges*

by Maurice Ravel

This music sounds like two animals talking.

What animals are they?

The Music Man

Danish Folk Song

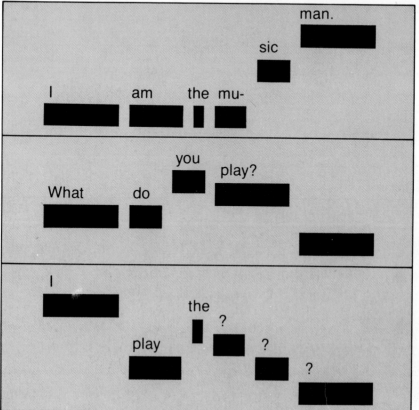

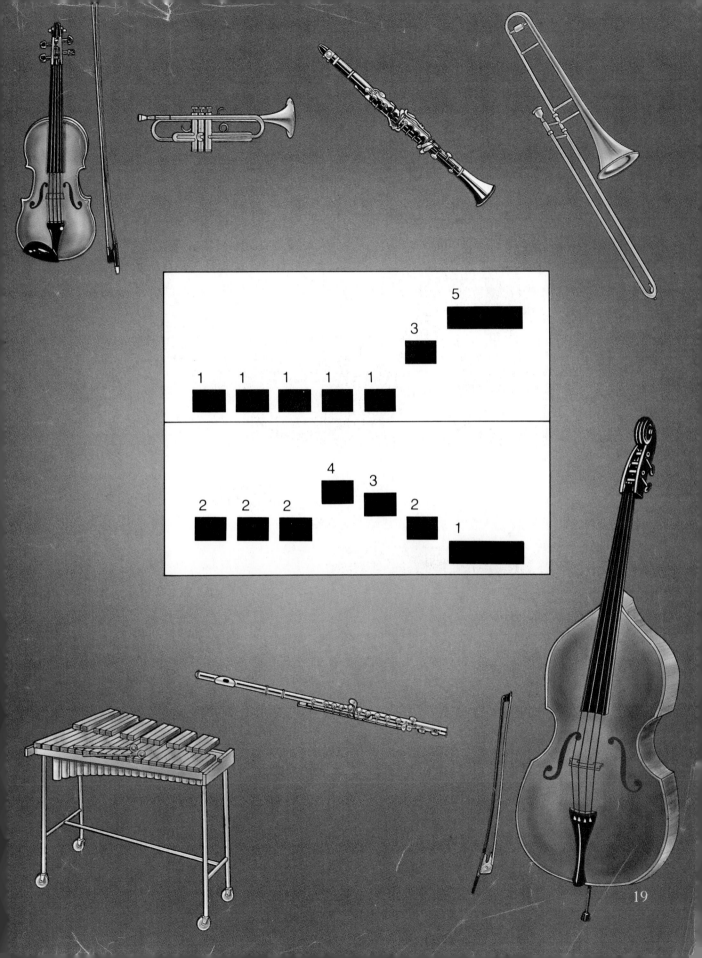

19

Little Red Caboose

American Folk Song

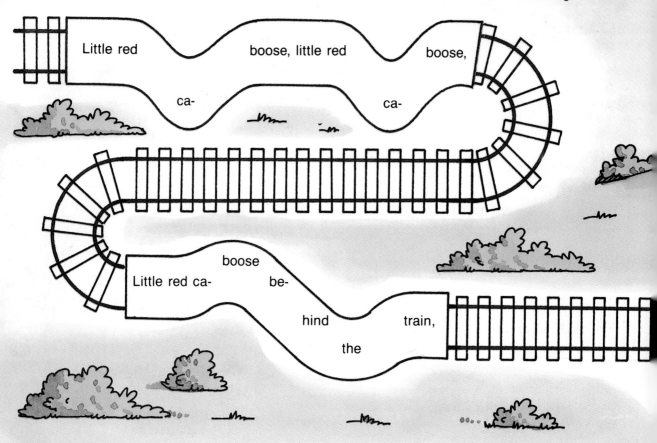

Little red ca-boose, little red ca-boose, Little red ca-boose be-hind the train,

Make your train song sound like this:

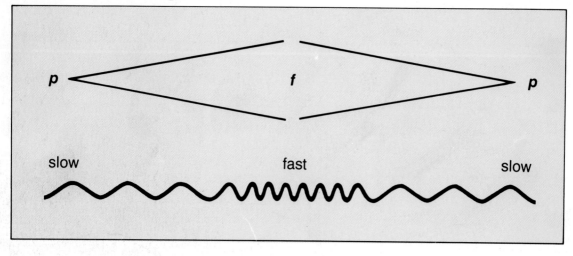

p   f   p

slow   fast   slow

Smokestack on its back, rumblin' down the track,

Little red ca-boose be-hind the train.

21

I Have a Duck

Poem by B. A.

I have a duck.
My duck is soft.

I have a duck.
My duck is yellow.

I have a duck.
My duck says, "Quack! Quack!"

I have a duck.
I just love my duck.

See the Little Ducklings

German Folk Song

Follow the ducks.
They show how the melody goes
up, down, or remains the same.

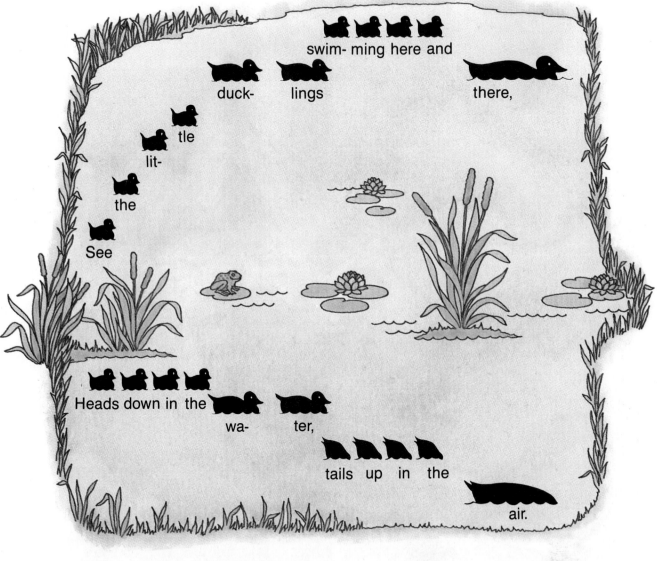

swim- ming here and

duck-   lings   there,

tle

lit-

the

See

Heads down in the   wa-   ter,

tails up in the

air.

Make up parts of the song.

All Sing: All Sing: All Sing:

Your song   Your song

Never Argue with a Bee

Words and Music by Malvina Reynolds

Introduction:

Buzz

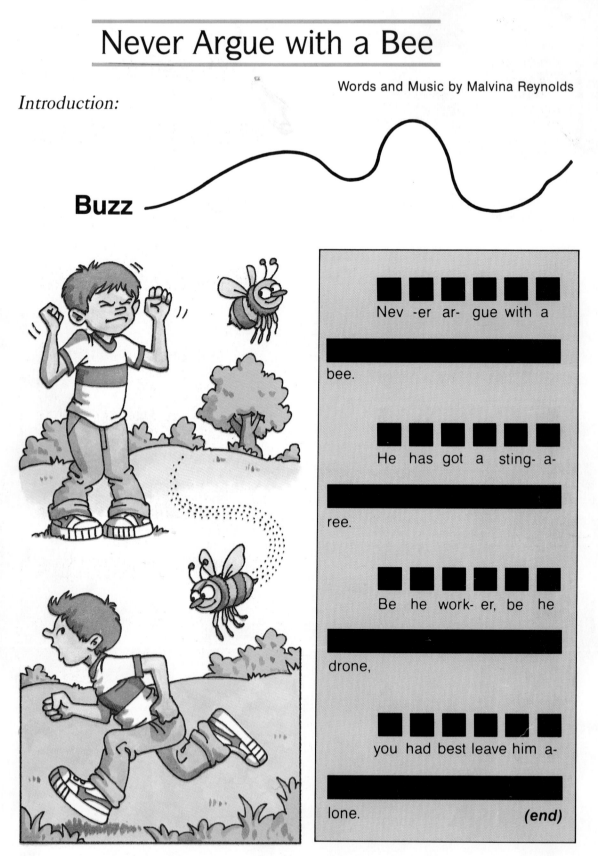

Nev -er ar- gue with a bee.

He has got a sting-a- ree.

Be he work- er, be he drone,

you had best leave him a- lone.

(end)

■ ■ ■ ■ ■ ■
He has got his work to

do,

■ ■ ■ ■ ■ ■
get- ting hon -ey from the

tree.

■ ■ ■ ■ ■ ■
If you know what's good for

you,

■ ■ ■ ■ ■ ■
do not ar- gue with a

bee.

(Go back to the beginning)

Closing:

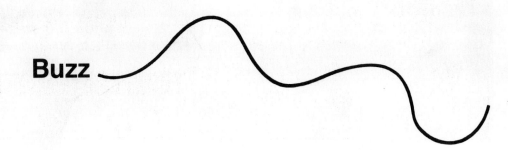

Buzz

25

Down by the Seashore

Words adapted by B. A.

American Ballad

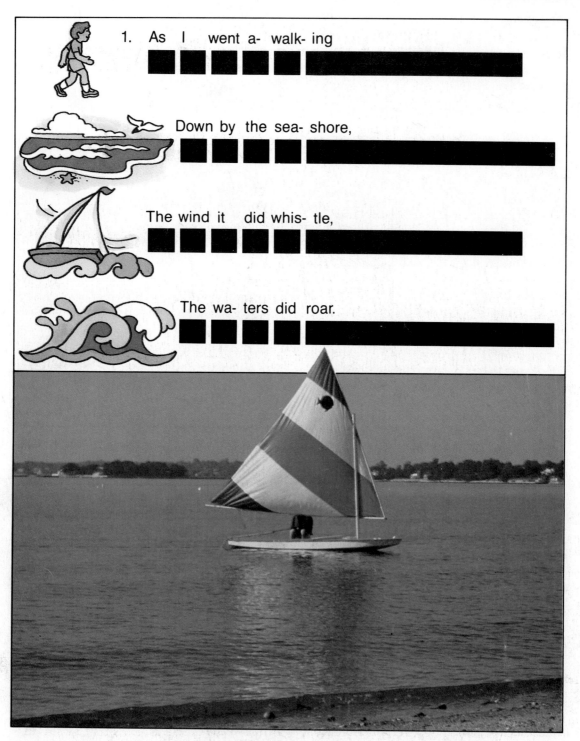

1. As I went a- walk- ing

Down by the sea- shore,

The wind it did whis- tle,

The wa- ters did roar.

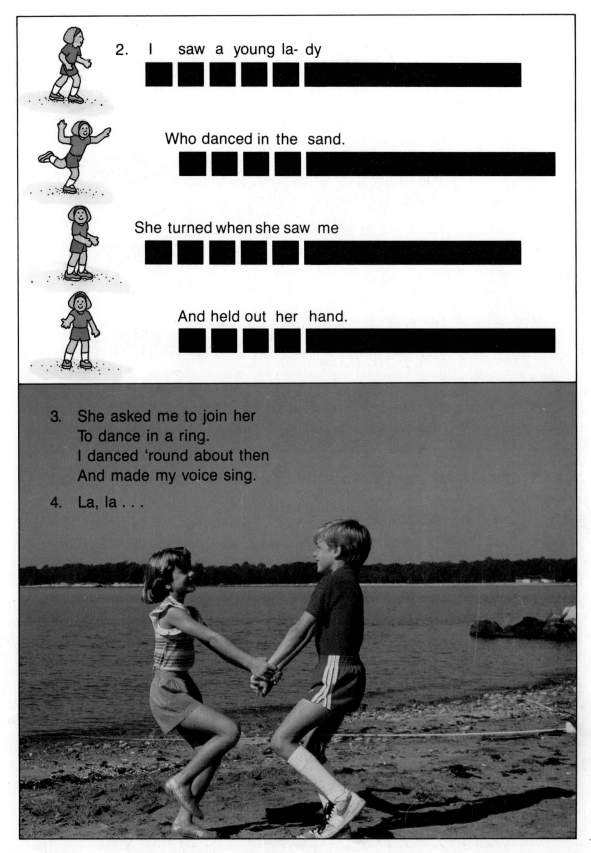

2. I saw a young la- dy

█ █ █ █ █ █████

Who danced in the sand.

█ █ █ █ █████

She turned when she saw me

█ █ █ █ █ █████

And held out her hand.

█ █ █ █ █████

3. She asked me to join her
To dance in a ring.
I danced 'round about then
And made my voice sing.

4. La, la . . .

27

Mary Mack

Verse 1 adapted by Ella Jenkins
Verses 2 and 3 traditional

Melody by Ella Jenkins

Move with the beat.

1. Ma-ry   Mack,   dressed in   black,

   Sil-ver   but-tons   down her back.

   Hi-   o!   Hi-   o!

   Hi-o!   Hi-o!   Hi-   o!

2. Asked her mother for fifteen cents to
   See the elephants jump the fence.
   Hi-o! Hi-o!
   Hi-o! Hi-o! Hi-o!

3. Jumped so high they touched the sky,
   Never came back till the fourth of July.
   Hi-o! Hi-o!
   Hi-o! Hi-o! Hi-o!

28

Play the bells
while you sing.

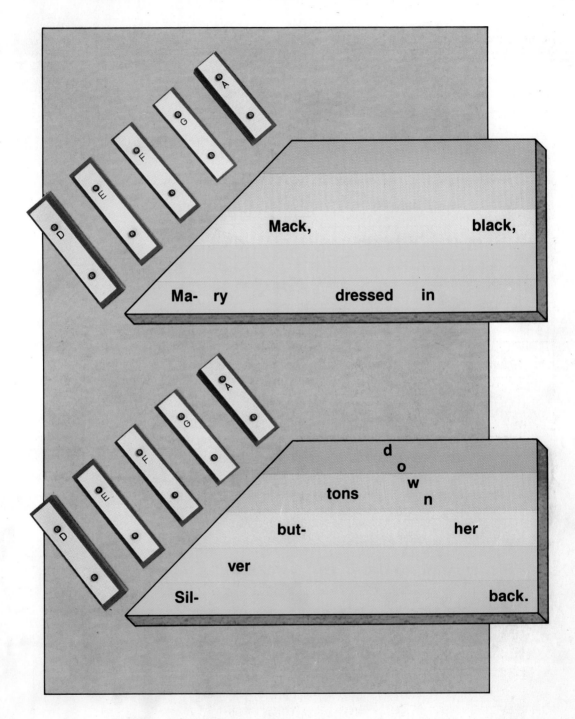

Which bells will you use to play "Hi-o"?
Play the whole song.

I've a Pair of Fishes

Words by J. Lilian Vandevere

Jewish Folk Tune

Verse 1

I've a pair of fish- es, fish- es.

They are washing dish- es, dish- es.

This is in- deed a wonder. See the fishes washing dishes.

This is quite a won- der, This is quite a won- der.

Verse 2

I've a pair of fox- es, fox- es.

They are build- ing box- es, box- es.

This is in- deed a won- der. See the fox- es build- ing box- es.

This is quite a won- der, This is quite a won- der.

31

Michael Finnegan

Traditional

★ **Start here** There was an old man Named Michael Finnegan. He had whiskers On his chinnegan. Along came the wind And blew them in again. Poor old Michael Finnegan! Begin again. There was an old man Named Michael Finnegan. He kicked up An awful dinnegan Because they would not Let him sing again. Poor old Michael Finnegan! Begin again.

Silly Rhymes

Rhyme 1

6
8

Look at the bees   fly | in- to the hive,

Tap:

One,   two, | three, four, ?

Rhyme 2

6
8

Wil- low- y Wan- da is | dressed in   blue,

She will be hap- py ? | ?   ?   ?

Rhyme 3

6
8

Mic- o- ry, Mac- o- ry, | John-ny and me

Went   ?

The Storm

The Train from Almendral

Children's Game from Uruguay

On the long rail of i - ron, the train from Al-men - dral

Goes a - puff - ing down the trail, With a

Chee-kee, chee-kee cha, Chee-kee, chee-kee cha.

Chee-kee, chee-kee cha, Chee-kee, chee-kee cha.

Play Phrase 3 and Phrase 4.
Use these bells.

Hocky Tocky Oombah

Camp Song

People like to sing this song around a campfire.

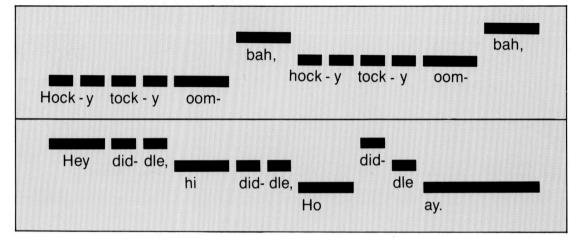

Hock - y tock - y oom- bah, hock - y tock - y oom- bah,

Hey did- dle, hi did- dle, Ho did- dle ay.

36

Some Tools of the Trade

A carpenter uses
    a hammer,
    nails, and a saw
to build things out of wood.

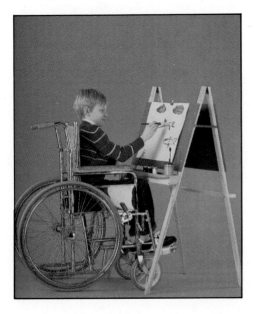

An artist uses
    paints
    and brushes
to make pictures .

A composer uses
    rhythm, melody,
    and instruments
to make music.

Use long and short sounds to make your composition.

■ ■ ■ ■ ■ ■ ■   ■ ■ ■ ■

What instrument will you use?

In the Hall of the Mountain King

from *Peer Gynt Suite No. 1*

by Edvard Grieg

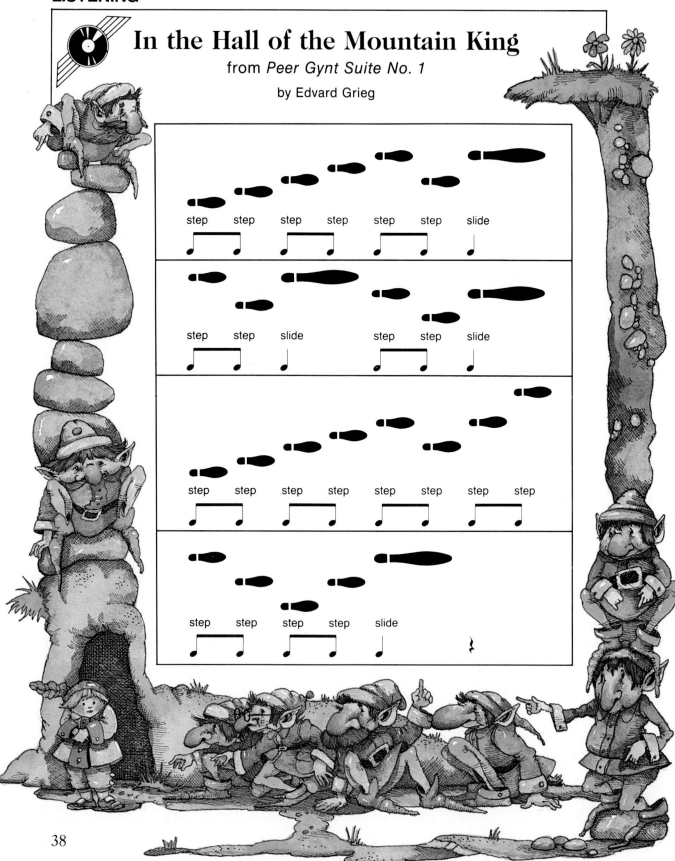

Does this music get—

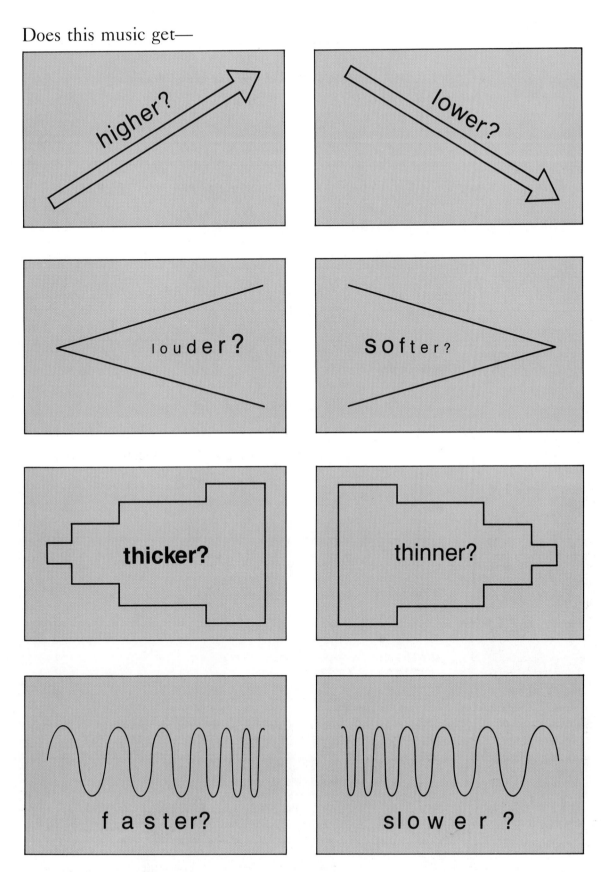

higher?

lower?

louder?

softer?

thicker?

thinner?

faster?

slower?

Sally Down the Alley

Traditional Play-Party Song

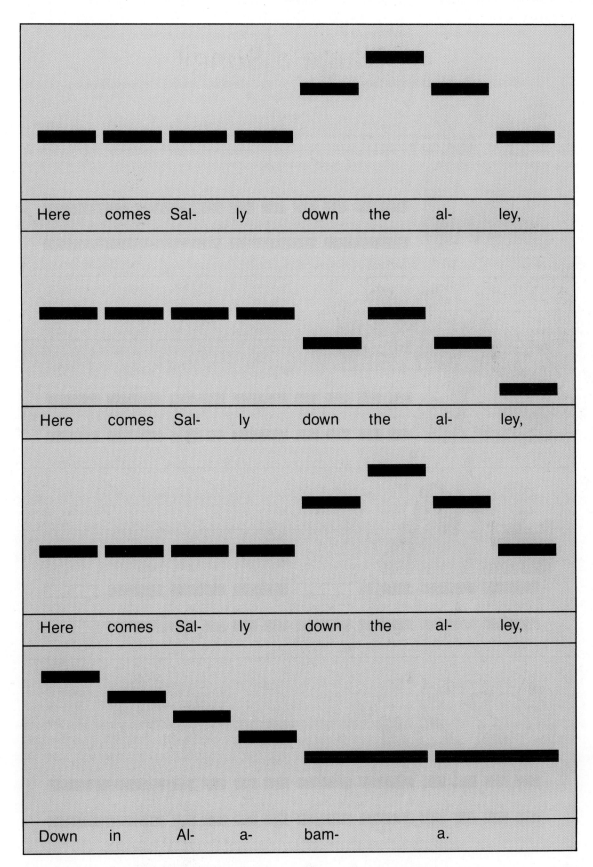

Name a Song

Rocky Mountain

Southern Folk Song

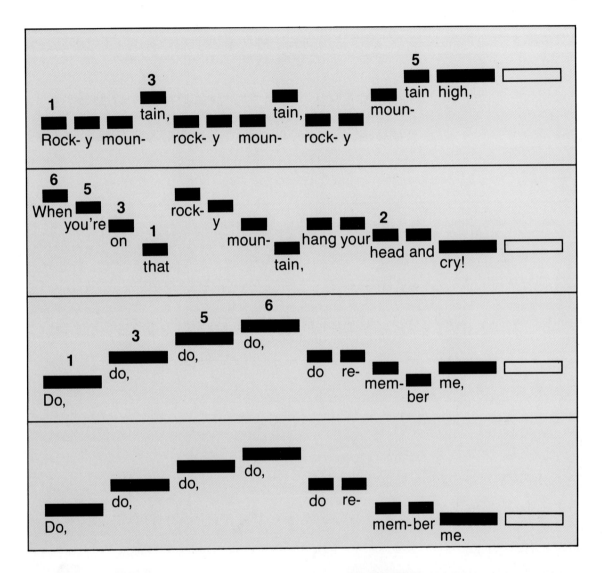

Phrase 1

Phrases 2, 3, and 4

Hot Dog

Camp Song

A Riddle

Higher than a house,

higher than a tree.

Oh! What- ever can that be?

Hi-ho for Mary-oh

Old English Folk Song

Chant the rhythm at the top of these two pages.

Play and sing this melody.

Ma-
ry   ry-
Ma-   mer-ry, mer-   oh,
for   ry-
Hi- ho   oh,

46

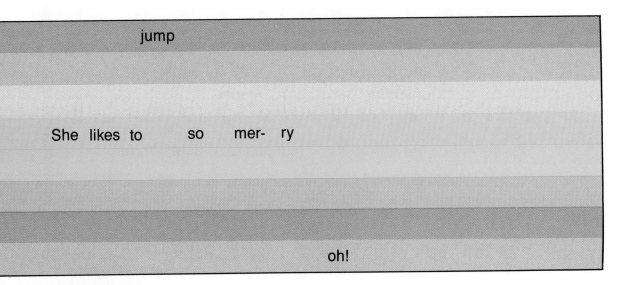

jump

She likes to   so   mer-   ry

oh!

LISTENING

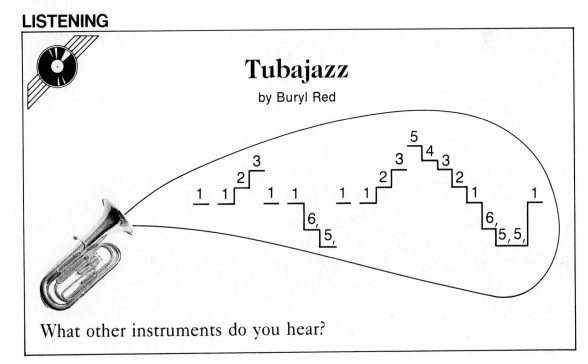

Tubajazz
by Buryl Red

1   1   2   3   1   1   6,   5,   1   1   2   3   5   4   3   2   1   6,   5, 5,   1

What other instruments do you hear?

Animal Song

American Folk Song

Al - li - ga - tor, mon - key, an - te - lope, cat,

Rat - tle - snake, buf - fa - lo, moun-tain goat, bat.

1. Al - li - ga - tor, mon - key, an - te - lope, cat,
2. Drom - e - dar - y, os - trich, whip-poor - will, moose,

Rat - tle - snake, buf - fa - lo, moun-tain goat, bat.
Kan - ga - roo, wol - ver - ine, guin - ea pig, goose.

3. Bunny rabbit, 'possum,
   porcupine, shark,
Chickadee, prairie dog,
   elephant, lark.

Up the Hickory

American Folk Song

Here is a picture of silence:

Can you play this game of sound and silence?

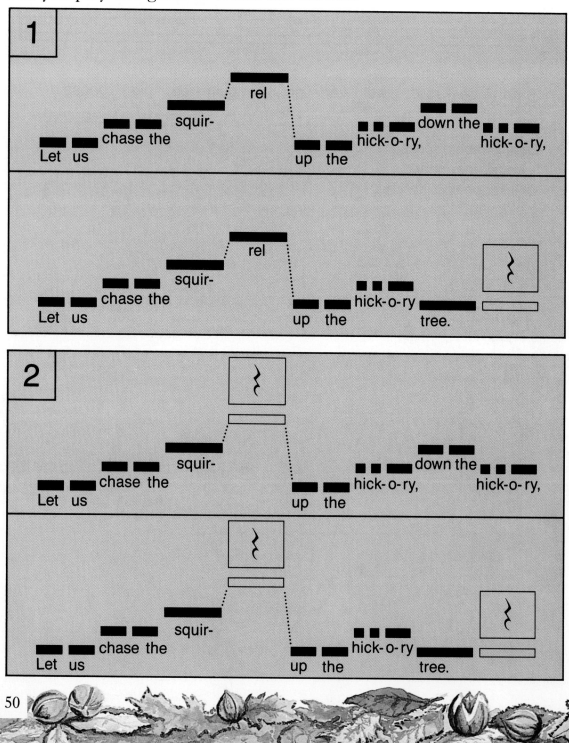

1

rel
squir-
chase the
Let us
up the
hick-o-ry,
down the
hick-o-ry,

rel
squir-
chase the
Let us
up the
hick-o-ry
tree.

2

squir-
chase the
Let us
up the
hick-o-ry,
down the
hick-o-ry,

squir-
chase the
Let us
up the
hick-o-ry
tree.

3

Let us chase the

up the hick-o-ry, down the hick-o-ry,

Let us chase the

up the hick-o-ry tree.

4

Let us

up the hick-o-ry, down the hick-o-ry,

Let us

up the hick-o-ry tree.

I Should Like to Go to Texas

Traditional

Read a rhythm.

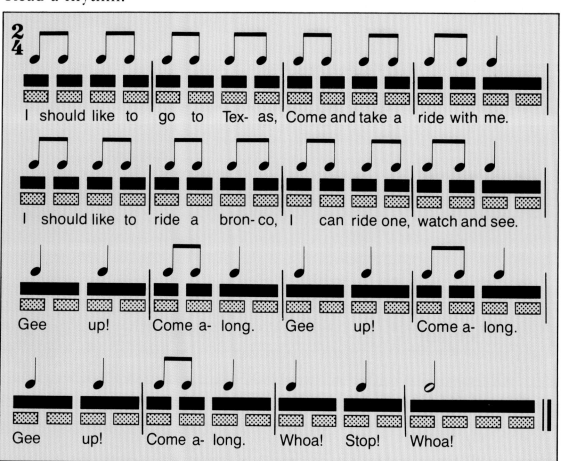

I should like to go to Tex- as, Come and take a ride with me.

I should like to ride a bron- co, I can ride one, watch and see.

Gee up! Come a- long. Gee up! Come a- long.

Gee up! Come a- long. Whoa! Stop! Whoa!

Follow a melody.

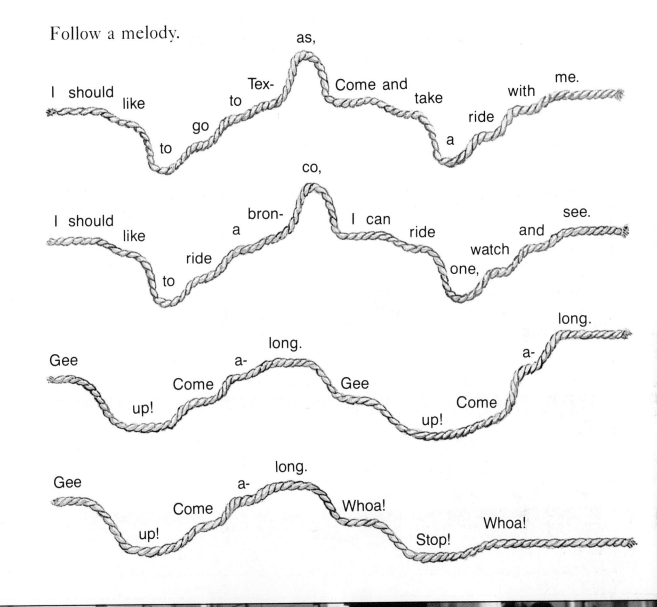

I should like to go to Tex- as, Come and take a ride with me.

I should like to ride a bron- co, I can ride one, watch and see.

Gee up! Come a- long. Gee up! Come a- long.

Gee up! Come a- long. Whoa! Stop! Whoa!

One Potato, Two Potatoes

Children's Chant

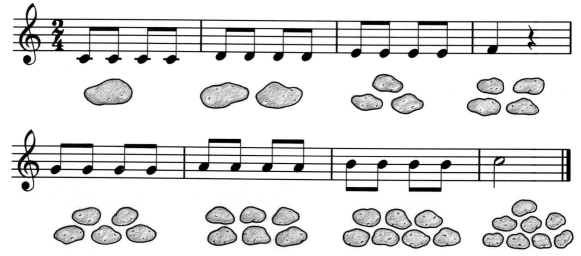

Who Has the Penny?

Traditional Children's Song

```
      3
    2
1 1       1
Who has the pen - ny?
```
I have the pen - ny.

```
        5
    3  4
3 3
Who has the key?
```
I have the key.

```
      1'
    7
  6
5         5
Who has the thim - ble?
```
I have the thim-ble.

```
3
    2 2
        1
Please let us see.
```
Please let us see.

Home Tone Game

Play the game.

Bell Player

First play the bell
that stands alone.

Play other bells,
then return to
the first bell.

Movers

Stand still when you hear
that bell played.

Move when you hear
the others.

Join into the Game

Additional words and music adaptation
by Paul Campbell (The Weavers)

A song has a **home tone**.

Tune up around the **home tone**.

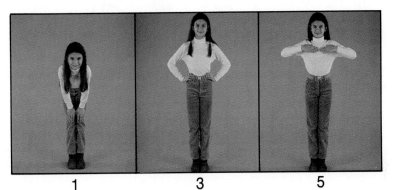

            1   3   5

Play a new game.

Move with the melody.

Stop each time you hear the **home tone**,

    then clap: ♩ ♩

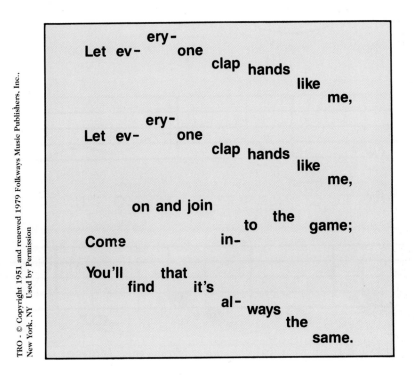

Let ev- ery- one clap hands like me,

Let ev- ery- one clap hands like me,

Come on and join in- to the game;

You'll find that it's al- ways the same.

The Mickey Mouse March

Words and music by Jimmie Dodd

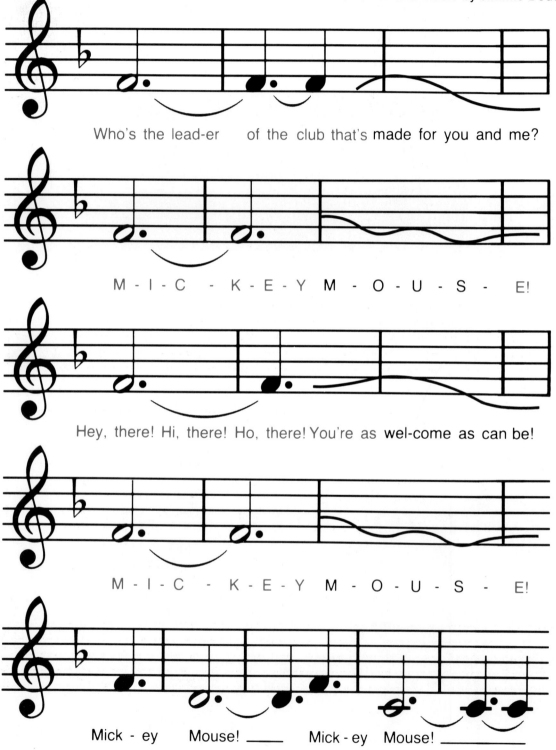

Who's the lead-er   of the club that's made for you and me?

M - I - C - K - E - Y M - O - U - S - E!

Hey, there! Hi, there! Ho, there! You're as wel-come as can be!

M - I - C - K - E - Y M - O - U - S - E!

Mick - ey   Mouse! ____   Mick - ey   Mouse! ____

For - ev-er let us hold our ban-ner high! _____

Come a-long and sing a song and join the jam-bor - ee!

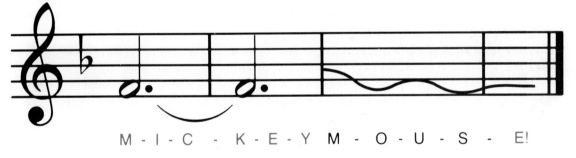

M - I - C - K - E - Y M - O - U - S - E!

In the Evening Moonlight

Traditional French Folk Song

Follow the pictures of short and long sounds.

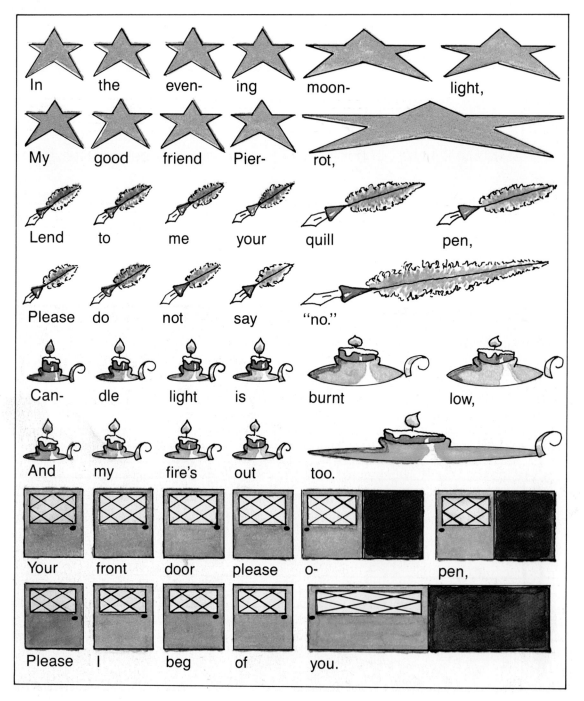

In the even- ing moon- light,

My good friend Pier- rot,

Lend to me your quill pen,

Please do not say "no."

Can- dle light is burnt low,

And my fire's out too.

Your front door please o- pen,

Please I beg of you.

In the eve-ning moon-light, My good friend Pier - rot,

Lend to me your quill pen, Please do not say "no."

Can-dle light is burnt low, And my fire's out too,

Your front door please o - pen, Please I beg of you.

The Happy River

French Folk Song

Hear the hap - py riv - er sing - ing, sing - ing,

Hear the hap - py riv - er sing - ing as it flows.

62

Add an accompaniment.

Wind chimes
or triangle

Resonator
bells

gent - ly   flow - ing

Review 2

One More River

College Song

Verse

1. Old No - ah built him - self an ark,

There's one more riv - er to cross.

He built it all of hick - ory bark,

There's one more riv - er to cross.

Refrain

One more riv - er, and that's the riv - er of Jor - dan.

One more riv - er, There's one more riv - er to cross. _____

64

2. The animals went in one by one,
   There's one more river to cross.
   The elephant chewin' a caraway bun,
   There's one more river to cross.
   Refrain

Sing the rest of the verses the same way you sang Verse 2.
Remember to sing the refrain at the end of each verse.

3. The animals went in two by two,
   The rhinoceros and the kangaroo.

4. The animals went in three by three,
   The bat, the bear, and the bumblebee.

5. The animals went in four by four,
   Old Noah got mad and hollered for more.

6. The animals went in five by five.
   Old Noah hollered, "You look alive."

7. The animals went in six by six,
   The hyena laughed at the monkey's tricks.

8. The animals went in seven by seven,
   Says the ant to the elephant, "Who are you shovin'?"

9. The animals went in eight by eight,
   Old Noah hollered, "It's getting late."

10. The animals went in nine by nine,
    Old Noah hollered to cut that line.

11. The animals went in ten by ten,
    Old Noah blew his whistle then.

Three Blue Pigeons

Traditional

Three blue pi-geons,

Three blue pi-geons,

Three blue pi - geons

sit-ting on the wall.

Noah's Ark

Argentine Folk Song

Learn the rhythm.

No-ah's ark has room for all, Crea-tures fat and thin and tall,

No-ah's ark has room, you see, And one cor-ner just for me.

Learn the melody.

No-ah's ark has room for all, Crea-tures fat and thin and tall,

No-ah's ark has room, you see, And one cor-ner just for me.

Sing the rhythm and the melody.

No - ah's ark has room for all,

Crea - tures fat and thin and tall,

No - ah's ark has room, you see,

And one cor - ner just for me.

Play Melodies

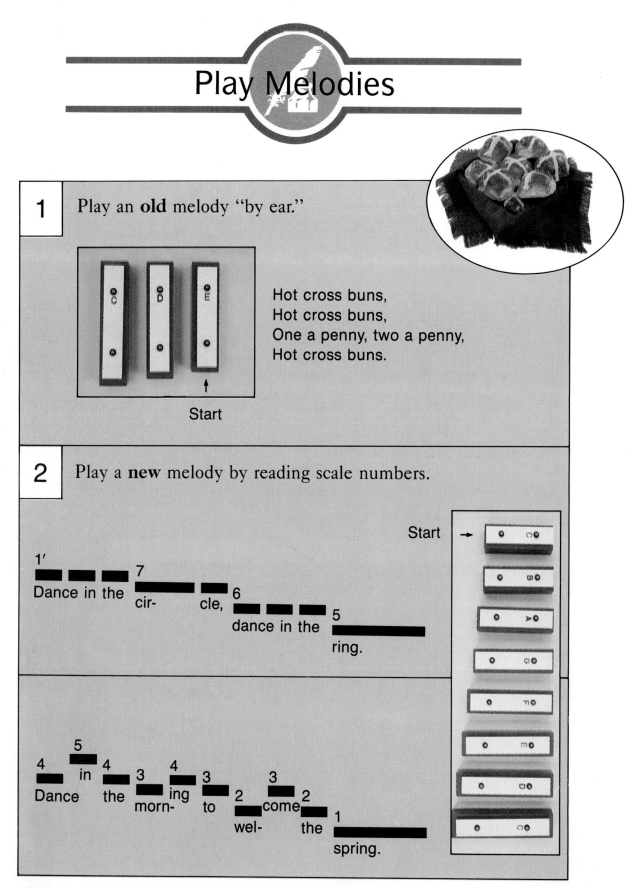

1 Play an **old** melody "by ear."

Hot cross buns,
Hot cross buns,
One a penny, two a penny,
Hot cross buns.

Start

2 Play a **new** melody by reading scale numbers.

Start

1′ Dance in the 7 cir- cle, 6 dance in the 5 ring.

4 Dance 5 in 4 the 3 morn- 4 ing 3 to 2 wel- 3 come 2 the 1 spring.

Rabbits

1 2 3   5

Traditional

↑
Start

Refrain
3

Rab-bits don't have tails at all,   Tails at all,   tails at all,

Rab-bits don't have tails at all,   Just wee pow-der   puffs.

(Say) Same song, first verse,
A little bit louder and a little bit worse!

1. Tails are barely there at all,
There at all, there at all,
Tails are barely there at all,
They're not good enough.
Refrain

(Say) Same song, second verse,
A little bit louder and a little bit worse!

2. Ears are longer than their tails,
Than their tails, than their tails,
Ears are longer than their tails,
Just wee bits of fluff.
Refrain

71

Trampin'

Spiritual

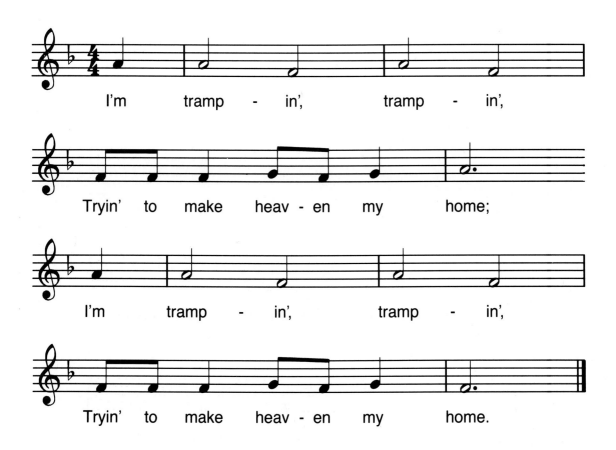

I'm tramp - in', tramp - in',

Tryin' to make heav - en my home;

I'm tramp - in', tramp - in',

Tryin' to make heav - en my home.

Follow these melody and harmony parts.

Melody

Harmony

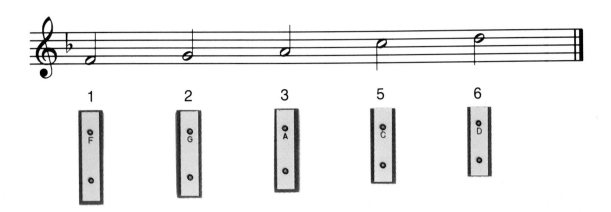

Pick a part to play.

Alto
glockenspiel
or
resonator bells

3   1

Tramp - in',   tramp - in',

Alto
xylophone
or
resonator bells

5   6

Tramp-in', tramp-in',   tramp-in' home.

Bass
xylophone
or
resonator bells

5
1

Let's   go   tramp - in'.

Little Tom Tinker

Traditional

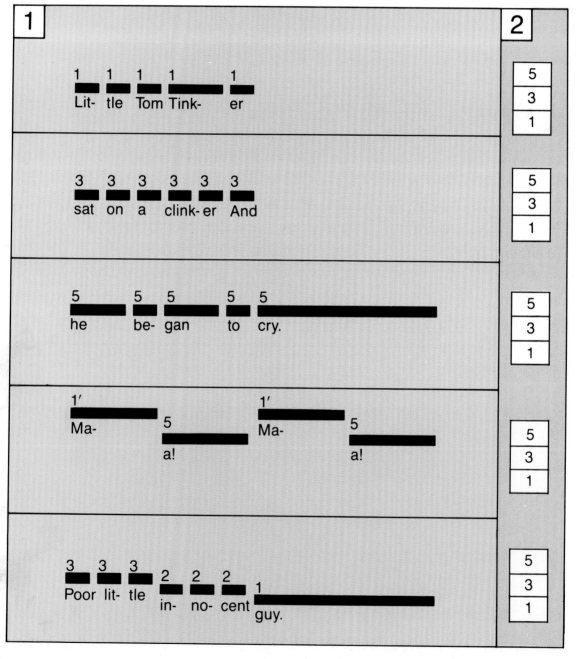

1

1	1	1	1		1
Lit-	tle	Tom	Tink-		er

3	3	3	3	3	3
sat	on	a	clink-	er	And

5		5	5		5	5
he		be-	gan		to	cry.

1'		1'	
Ma-	5	Ma-	5
	a!		a!

3	3	3	2	2	2	1
Poor	lit-	tle	in-	no-	cent	guy.

2

5
3
1

5
3
1

5
3
1

5
3
1

5
3
1

74

Sarabande

by Johann Pezel

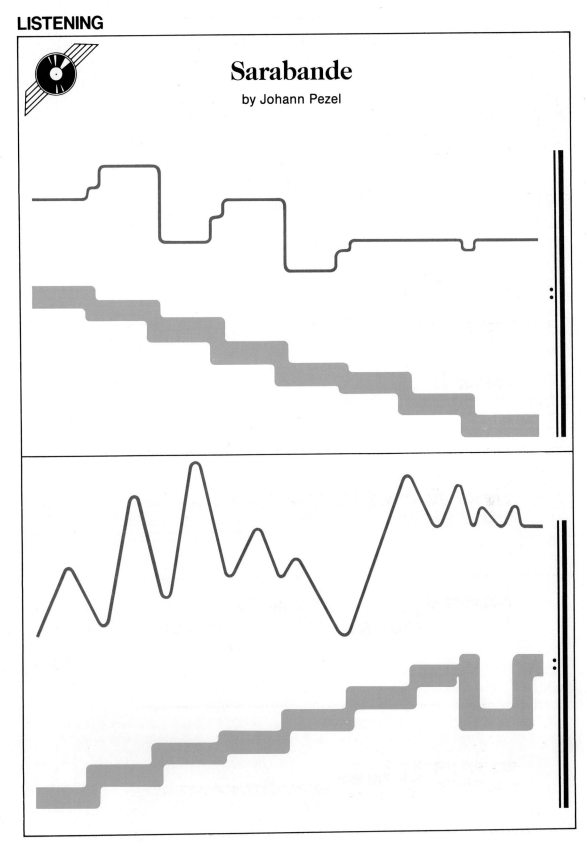

Charlie over the Ocean

Playground Game

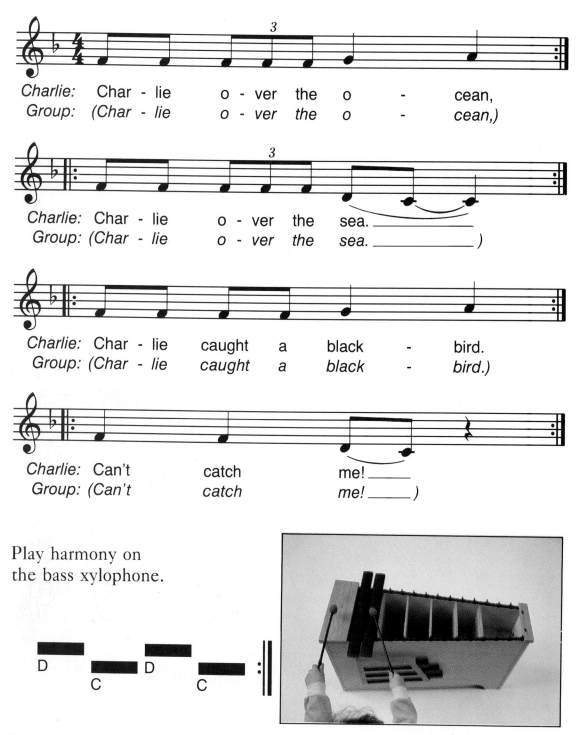

Charlie: Char - lie   o - ver   the   o - cean,
Group: (Char - lie   o - ver   the   o - cean,)

Charlie: Char - lie   o - ver   the   sea.
Group: (Char - lie   o - ver   the   sea.)

Charlie: Char - lie   caught   a   black - bird.
Group: (Char - lie   caught   a   black - bird.)

Charlie: Can't   catch   me!
Group: (Can't   catch   me!)

Play harmony on
the bass xylophone.

D   D
   C   C

Play two sounds
at the same time.

Play one sound
after another.

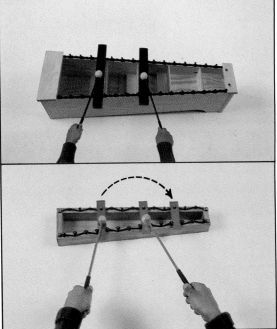

Play the autoharp.
Find low strings.

Find high strings.

Find this button.

F
Maj.

Press it down.

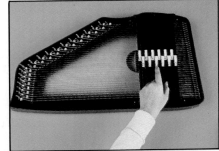

Strum the strings from
low to high.

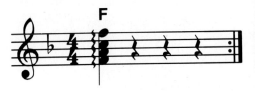

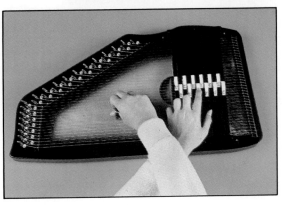

Pizza Pie

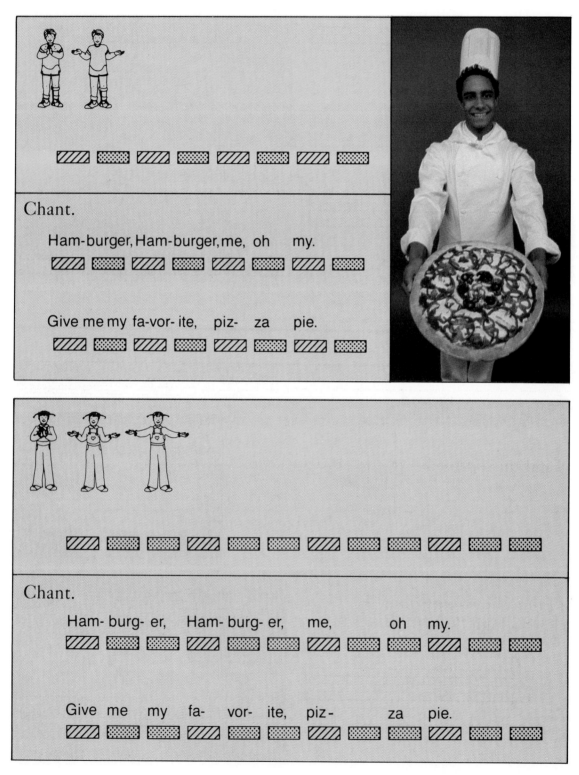

Chant.

Ham-burger, Ham-burger, me, oh my.

Give me my fa-vor- ite, piz- za pie.

Chant.

Ham- burg- er, Ham- burg- er, me, oh my.

Give me my fa- vor- ite, piz- za pie.

Which song matches each clapping pattern?

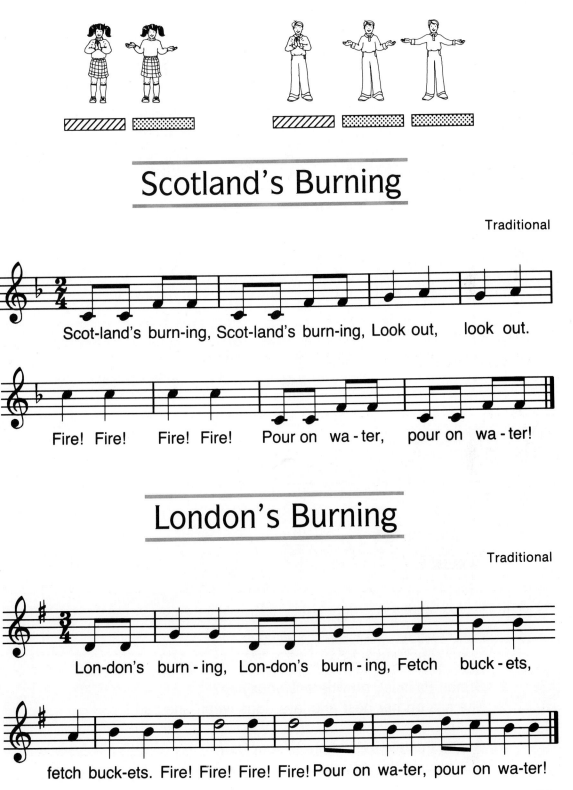

Scotland's Burning

Traditional

Scot-land's burn-ing, Scot-land's burn-ing, Look out, look out.

Fire! Fire! Fire! Fire! Pour on wa-ter, pour on wa-ter!

London's Burning

Traditional

Lon-don's burn-ing, Lon-don's burn-ing, Fetch buck-ets,

fetch buck-ets. Fire! Fire! Fire! Fire! Pour on wa-ter, pour on wa-ter!

Gretel, Pastetel

German Folk Song

Let's tune up.

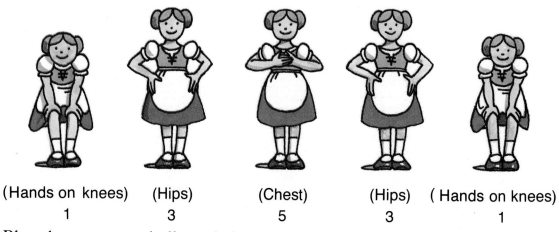

(Hands on knees)   (Hips)   (Chest)   (Hips)   (Hands on knees)
1   3   5   3   1

Play the resonator bells and sing.

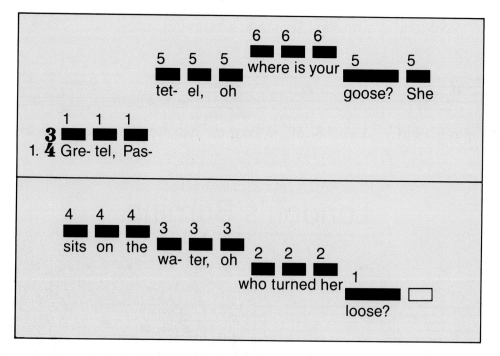

2. Gretel, Pastetel, oh where is your hen?
   She sits on her nest and lays eggs when she can.

3. Gretel, Pastetel, oh where is your cow?
   She stays in her stall but I can't milk her now.

Take away one beat from each bell's sounds.

What song did you just play?

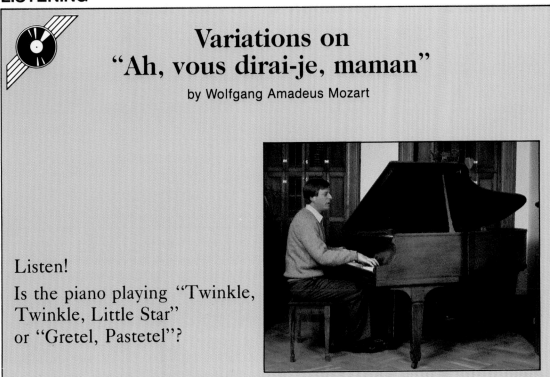

Variations on "Ah, vous dirai-je, maman"

by Wolfgang Amadeus Mozart

Listen!

Is the piano playing "Twinkle, Twinkle, Little Star" or "Gretel, Pastetel"?

81

The Night Was Creeping

by James Stephens

The Night was creeping
on the ground!

Until she reached the tree:
And then she covered it,

And stole again
along the grass
beside the wall!

She threw blackness
everywhere

Along the sky,
the ground,
the air,

But, no matter what she did
To everything that was without,
She could not put my candle out!

What Shall We Do on a Rainy Day?

Traditional

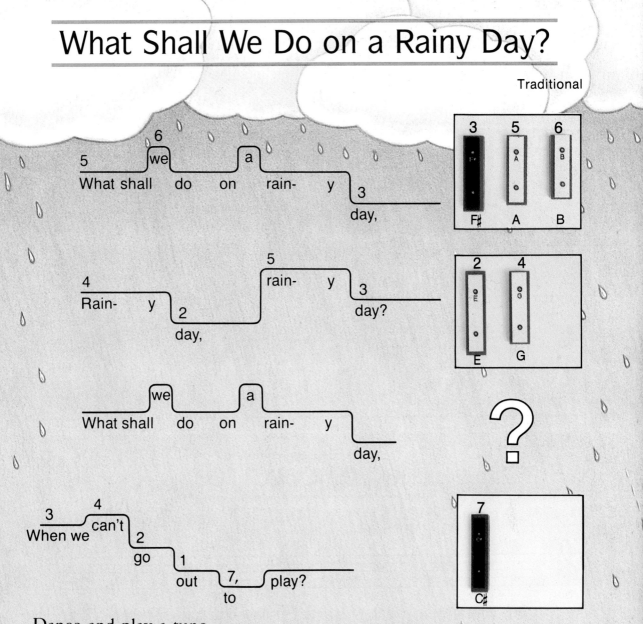

5 What shall 6 we do on rain- y 3 day,

4 Rain- y 2 day, 5 rain- y 3 day?

What shall we do on rain- a y day,

3 When we 4 can't 2 go 1 out 7, to play?

Dance and play a tune.

Song in the Night
by Carlos Salzedo

The Lollipop Tree

Words by Joe Darion

Music by George Kleinsinger

1. One fine day in ear-ly spring I played a fun-ny trick,

Out in the yard be - hind our house

I plant - ed a lol - li - pop stick,

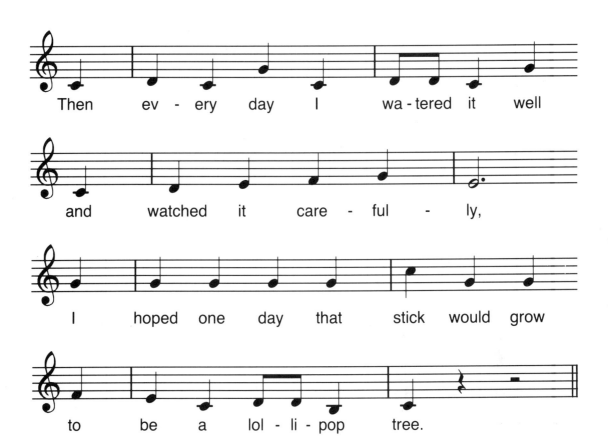

Then ev - ery day I wa - tered it well

and watched it care - ful - ly,

I hoped one day that stick would grow

to be a lol - li - pop tree.

Ha, ha, ha, Ho, ho, ho, What a sight to see,

Me and my lol - li - pop, lol - li - pop, lol - li - pop,

lol - li, lol - li, lol - li - pop tree.

2. Then one day I woke to find a very lovely
      sight,
   A tree all full of lollipops had grown in the
      dark of night,
   I sat beneath that wonderful tree and looked
      up with a grin,
   And when I opened up my mouth a pop
      would drop right in.

   Ha, ha, ha, Ho, ho, ho, What a place to be,
   Under a lollipop, lollipop, lollipop,
      lolli, lolli, lollipop tree.

3. Winter came and days grew cold as winter
      days will do,
   On my tree, my lovely tree, not one little
      lollipop grew;
   From every branch an icicle hung, the twigs
      were bare as bones,
   But when I broke the icicles off they turned
      to ice-cream cones.

   Ha, ha, ha, Ho, ho, ho, How I danced with
      glee,
   Under the lollipop, lollipop, lollipop,
      lolli, lolli, lollipop tree.

Jim Along, Josie

Traditional

Hey, Jim a - long,   Jim a - long, Jo - sie.

Hey, Jim a - long,   Jim a - long, Joe!

Hey, Jim a - long,   Jim a - long, Jo - sie.

The end

Hey, Jim a - long,   Jim a - long, Joe!

Face to the cen - ter.   Hands on your knees.

Go back to the beginning.

Clap three times and turn a - round, please!

89

Rique Ran

Latin American Folk Song

Find the instruments that play
only rhythm patterns . . .
the melody . . .
the harmony.

A - se - rrín, a - se - rrán,

All the woods-men of San Juan

Eat their cheese and eat their pan,

Those from Ri - que al - fe - ñi - que;

Those from Ro - que al - fon - do - que,

Ri - qui, ri - que, ri - qui ran.

Prince of Denmark March

by Jeremiah Clarke

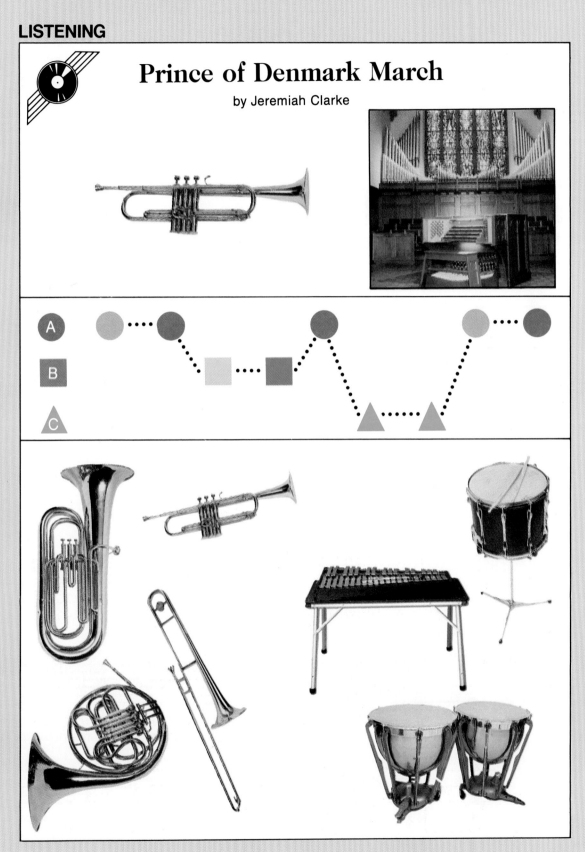

Black Horse

Words and music by
Malvina Reynolds

Refrain

I want to ride on the black horse,

the black horse, the black horse,

Dad - dy, put me up on the black horse,

Go to verse. | *The end*

'cause he's the one for me. me.

Verse

1. Oh, the black horse lives on the mer - ry - go - round

that plays a march - ing song,

And it's just like be-ing in a big pa-rade

that goes on all day long.

The mu-sic starts and a-way we go,

and the black horse gal-lops and the rest go slow,

'cause he's the one in the ver-y front row,

Go back to the beginning.

and he's the one for me.

2. Oh, the white horse is a beautiful horse
   But he doesn't gallop at all.
   And the little red wagon's only made
   For children very small.
   But people come from all over town
   To see the black horse go up and down.
   And I wave my hat when we come around,
   And he's the one for me.
   Refrain

Doctor Foster

Mother Goose Rhyme

Music by Mary Tolbert

Doc - tor Fos - ter   went to Glos - ter

in   a   show - er   of   rain;

He   stepped in a pud - dle up   to his mid - dle

and   nev - er went there a - gain.

Use these bells or glockenspiel bars.

Play these patterns.

① 1' 5 1' 5
Drip, drop, drip, drop,

② 6-6 6 5 5 | 1
Nev-er went there a - gain. _____

Doc - tor   Fos - ter   went   to   Glos - ter

in   a   show-er   of   rain;

He stepped in a   pud-dle up   to his   mid-dle

and   nev - er went   there   a   -   gain. _____

Use these glockenspiel
bars or bells.

C D   G   C

Play these patterns.

① 1'   1' | 5   5 :| ② 1   1   1 | 2   2   2 :|
Doc -   tor Fos -   ter,   stepped in   a   pud- dle,   He

95

LISTENING

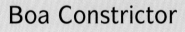

Boa Constrictor

Words and music by Shel Silverstein

I'm being eaten by a boa constrictor,
A boa constrictor, a boa constrictor, a boa constrictor,
I'm being eaten by a boa constrictor,
And I don't like it one bit.

Wha-da-ya know, it's nibblin' my toe;
Oh gee, it's up to my knee;
Oh my, it's up to my thigh;
Oh fiddle, it's up to my middle;
Oh heck, it's up to my neck;
Oh dread, it's up to my mm-mm-mm-m. . .

All the Pretty Little Horses

American Folk Song

Find this sign: :‖

Listen to the recording.

What does the sign mean?

1. Hush - a - by,   don't you cry,
2. When you wake,   you shall have

Fine

Go to sleep - y, lit - tle ba - by.
All the pret - ty lit - tle hors - es:

Blacks and bays, dap - ples and grays,

D.C. al Fine

Coach and six - a lit - tle hors - es.

These pictures show the form of the song.

What do they tell you about that form?

A   A   B   A

Sailing
from *Harbor Vignettes*

by Herbert Donaldson

Begin here.

Is this music peaceful? noisy? loud? soft?

Come Sailing with Me

Words adapted by F.W.

Italian Folk Song

1. Come sail - ing with me, _____
2. Come sail - ing with me, _____

Come sail - ing with me, _____
Come sail - ing with me, _____

Float-ing so peace-ful - ly down to the sea,
Fol - low-ing white-caps that dance mer - ri - ly,

Come sail - ing with me. _____
Come sail - ing with me. _____

Carnival of the Animals
by Camille Saint-Saëns

Can you find each animal described in the music?

Which animal is your favorite?

Will the music for your new animal be
loud? soft?   fast? slow?   high? low?   in 2s? in 3s?

The Snake

Words and music by Marshall Barron

Slowly, softly

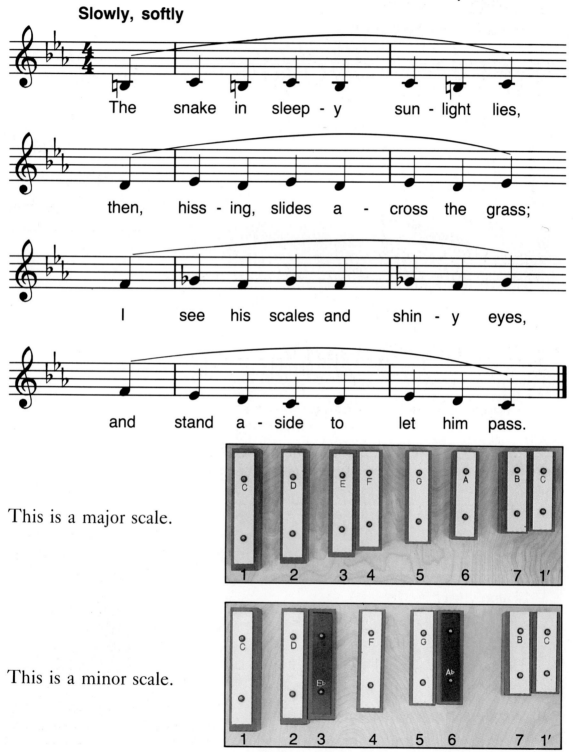

The snake in sleep - y sun - light lies,

then, hiss - ing, slides a - cross the grass;

I see his scales and shin - y eyes,

and stand a - side to let him pass.

This is a major scale.

This is a minor scale.

Three Craw

Scottish Folk Song

Steadily, medium loud

1. Three craw sat up-on a wa',

Sat up-on a wa',

Sat up-on a wa';

Three craw sat up-on a wa'

On a cold and frost-y morn - ing.

2. First craw couldna find his maw,
   Couldna find his maw,
   Couldna find his maw;
   First craw couldna find his maw
   On a cold and frosty morning.

3. Second craw couldna find his paw, . . .

4. Third craw couldna een say "caw," . . .

5. Fourth craw warna there at aw, . . .

6. That's aw I hear about the craw, . . .

103

Lavender's Blue

English Folk Song

1. Lav - en - der's blue, dil - ly, dil - ly, lav - en - der's green,
2. Call up your men, dil - ly, dil - ly, set them to work,

When I am King, dil - ly, dil - ly, you shall be Queen;
Some with a rake, dil - ly, dil - ly, some with a fork;

Who told you so? dil - ly, dil - ly, who told you so?
Some to make hay, dil - ly, dil - ly, some to thresh corn,

'Twas mine own heart, dil - ly, dil - ly, that told me so.
While you and I, dil - ly, dil - ly, keep our-selves warm.

Allemande
by Claude Gervaise

Hallelu

Israeli Folk Song

Hal -le -lu -jah, hal -le -lu -jah, hal -le -lu -jah, hal -le -lu!

Hal -le -lu -jah, hal -le -lu -jah, hal -le -lu -jah, hal -le -lu!

Hal -le -lu -jah, hal -le -lu, hal -le -lu -jah, hal -le -lu!

Hal -le -lu -jah, hal -le -lu -jah, hal -le -lu -jah, hal -le -lu!

Tambourine

Hand drum

Finger cymbals

Composers at Work

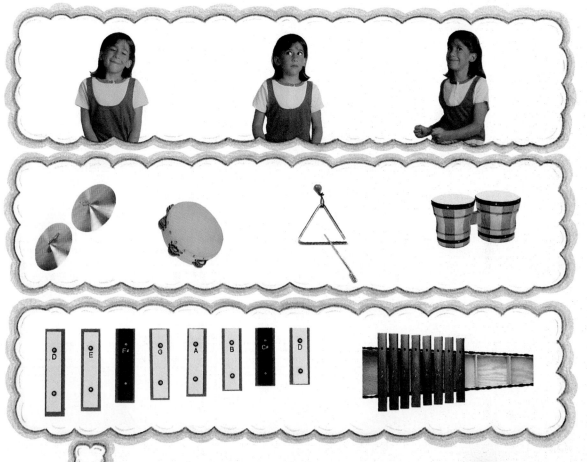

See-Saw Sacradown

Traditional

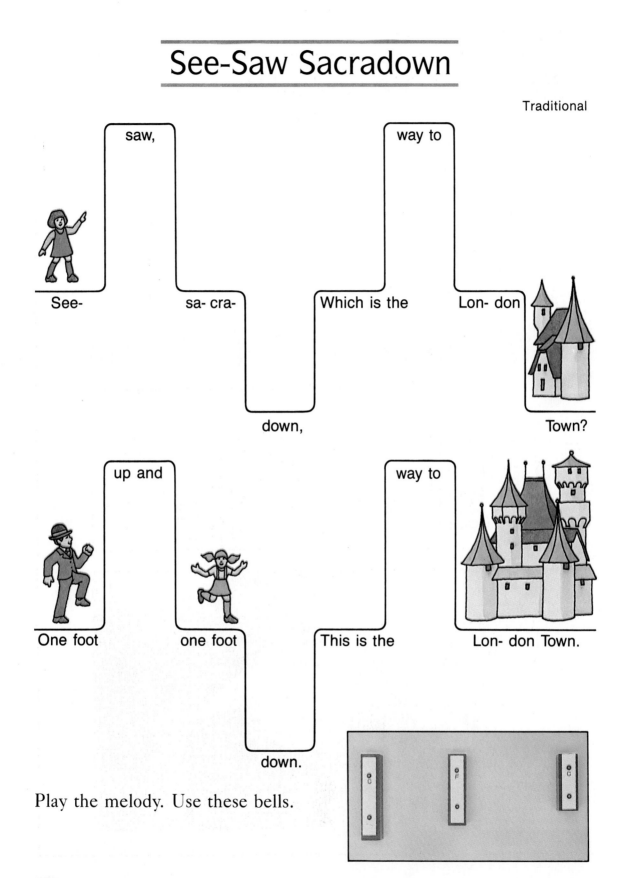

saw,

way to

See-

sa- cra-

Which is the

Lon- don

down,

Town?

up and

way to

One foot

one foot

This is the

Lon- don Town.

down.

Play the melody. Use these bells.

The Aeolian Harp
by Henry Cowell

You can hear one sound at a time make a **melody**.

You can hear many sounds at a time make **harmony**.

Follow the picture of melody and harmony.

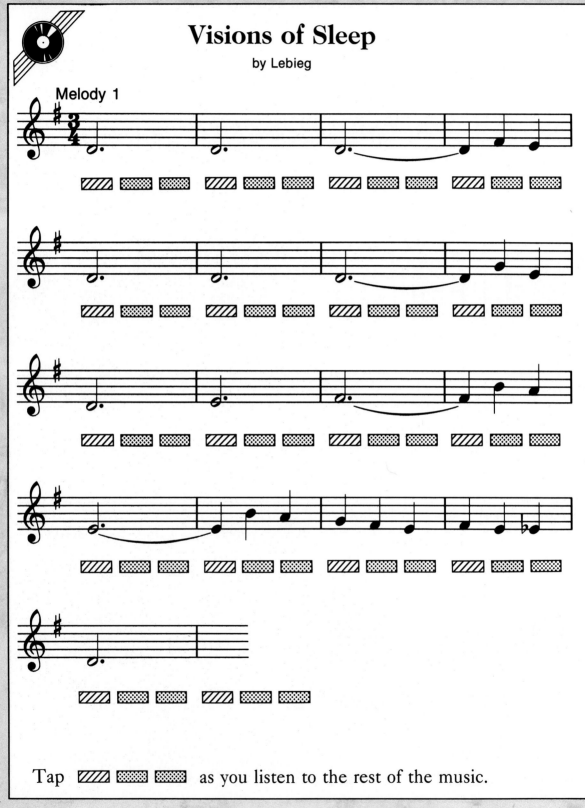

Melody 2

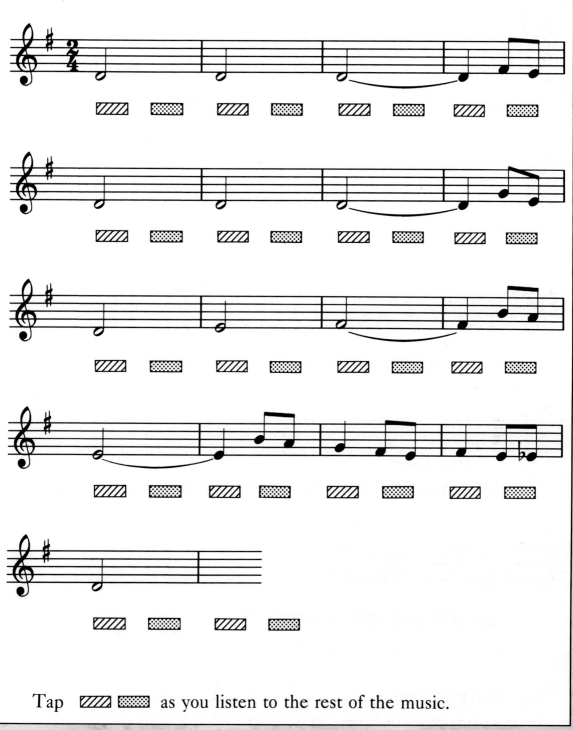

Tap as you listen to the rest of the music.

Read a Rhythm

Tap the rhythms.

Can you name these songs?

Song 1

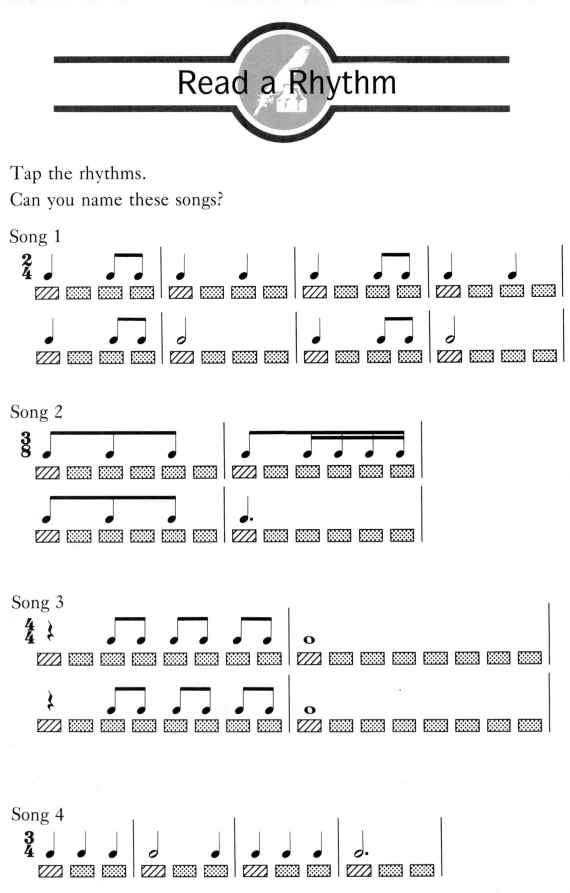

Song 2

Song 3

Song 4

Rain Song

Words Anonymous

Music by Irving Lowens

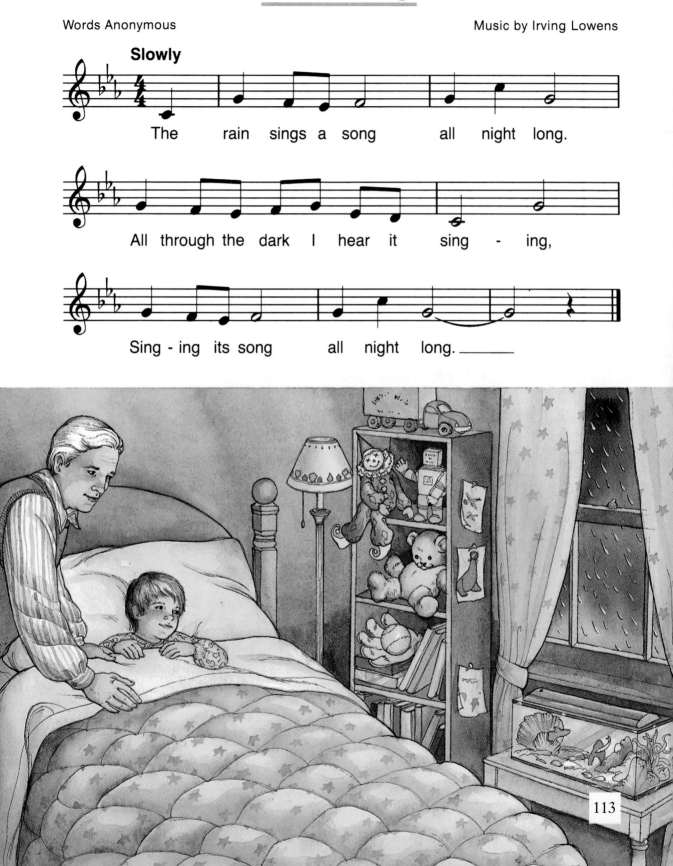

Slowly

The rain sings a song all night long.

All through the dark I hear it sing - ing,

Sing - ing its song all night long. _____

It's All Right to Cry

Words and music by Carol Hall

This is a very long song.

Follow the up-down note picture with your finger.

How many times do you hear the melody on this page?

1. It's all right to cry. Cry-ing gets the sad out of you.
2. Rain-drops from your eyes, Wash-ing all the mad out of you.
3. It's all right to know, Feel-ings come and feel-ings go, and

Fine

It's all right to cry. It might make you feel bet-ter.
Rain-drops from your eyes, It might make you feel bet-ter.
It's all right to cry. It might make you feel bet-ter.

It's all right to feel things though the feel-ings may be

strange. Feel-ings are such real things, And they

change and change and change. Sad and grump-y, Down in the dump-y,

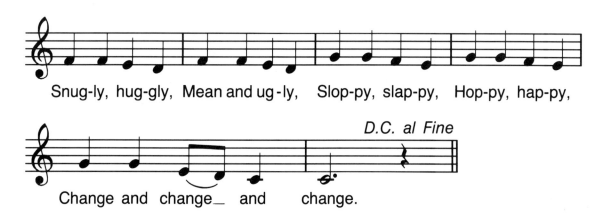

Snug-ly, hug-gly, Mean and ug-ly, Slop-py, slap-py, Hop-py, hap-py,

D.C. al Fine

Change and change_ and change.

Can you sing this song in a way that shows how you feel?

Will you always sing the same way?

Hear Musical Form

Listen to a march.

> How many parts does it have?
>
> Are some parts the same?
>
> Are some parts different?
>
> Which picture shows the same-different form?

See Musical Form

Look at the music on page 117.

> How many phrases do you see?
>
> Are some phrases the same?
>
> Are some phrases different?

Make a picture that shows

the same-different form of this song.

H-A-Double P-I-N-E-Double S

Words and music by Doug Nichol

Refrain

H - A - dou-ble P - I - N - E - dou-ble S,

Fine

H - A - dou-ble P - I - N - E - dou-ble S.

1. Hap - pi - ness is what we want for

ev - ery - one in the world.

Hap - pi - ness we'll try to make for

D.C. al Fine

ev - ery boy and girl And it's spelled

2. Let's all try to fill the world
   with love and unity.
Just remember happiness
   begins with you and me
And it's spelled . . .

117

Read a Melody

Look at the music on page 119.

1. When does the melody

| move by | move by | stay the |
| steps? | skips? | same? |

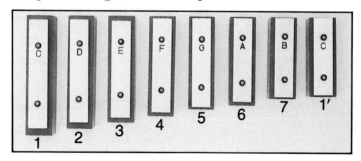

2. This melody starts on scale number 1.
   What are the numbers
   for the other notes in this song?

1 __ __ __ __ __ __

3. Which of these bells will you need
   to play the patterns given in Step 4?

4. Play 1-3-5-3-1.   Sing 1-3-5-3-1.
   Play 1'-5-3-1.   Sing 1'-5-3-1.

5. Sing the whole song.

118

The Choo Choo

Hungarian Children's Song

There's the choo choo, there's the choo choo, Ka - ni - zsa   line.

Ka - ni - zsa, oh,   Ka - ni - zsa, oh,   run-ning so   fine.

En - gi - neer   sits   in   the   cab   high,

Makes the choo choo, makes the choo choo rat - tle on   by.

If You Can't Say Something Nice

Words and music by
Richard M. and Robert B. Sherman

If you can't say some-thing nice, *Shhh!* say noth-ing.

Take a bit of good ad-vice, *Shhh!* say noth-ing.

Think of friend-ly things to say, That's the path to fol-low.

When you think un-friend-ly thoughts, Close your lips and swal-low!

If you think it   o-ver twice,   And you can't say some-thing nice,

Then   don't   say   an - y -thing at   all!   *Shhh!*

If I Were a Flower

Words and music
by Joseph and Nathan Segal

1. If I were a flow - er, ___ what do you think I'd see?

I'd see the sun and rain and clouds, all sur-round-ing me.

2. If I were a lit - tle bird, _ what do you think I'd see?
3. If I were a big black bug, _ what do you think I'd see?

I'd see my nest and moth-er bird wait-ing to feed me.
I'd see the dirt and big green trees

twice as big as me. 4. But I'm a child of the earth,

what do you think I see? I see from think-ing 'bout

what I'm   not   that I'm   glad just   to   be   me.

Play these patterns for Verses 1, 2, and 3.

Choose different instruments for each verse.

When will you choose instruments that are high? low?

Question

3 3 3 2   4 4 3

Answer

4   3   2   1

Three people may play patterns at the same time
for Verse 4.

Soprano metallophone

6   5   4   3   4   3   2   1

Bass xylophone

4   1   5   1

Soprano glockenspiel

6 4 5 3   4 2 1

123

Review 4

The Tree in the Wood

English Folk Song

1. All in ___ a ___ wood there grew a tree,
2. And on ___ this ___ tree there grew a limb,

The fin - est ___ tree you ev - er did see;

1. The tree was in the wood.
2. The limb was on the tree,
   The tree was in the wood.

Refrain

And the green leaves grew all a - round, a-round, a-round,

And the green leaves grew all a - round. ___

3. And on this limb there was a branch,
    The finest branch you ever did see;
    The branch was on the limb,
    The limb was on the tree,
    The tree was in the wood.
    Refrain

4. And on this branch there was a nest. *(Refrain)*
5. And in this nest there was an egg. *(Refrain)*
6. And in this egg there was a bird. *(Refrain)*
7. And on this bird there was a wing. *(Refrain)*
8. And on this wing there was a feather. *(Refrain)*

Read this harmony part.

More Music To Explore

Hey Diddle Diddle

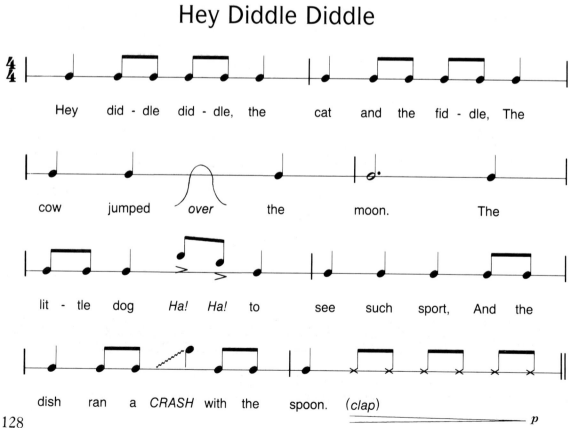

Hey did - dle did - dle, the cat and the fid - dle, The

cow jumped *over* the moon. The

lit - tle dog *Ha! Ha!* to see such sport, And the

dish ran a *CRASH* with the spoon. (*clap*)

Tell Me Why

Words by Oscar Hammerstein II

Music by Richard Rodgers

Tell me why the sky is filled with mu - sic,
Di - tes moi pour-quoi la vie est bel - le,

Tell me why we fly on clouds a - bove.
Di - tes moi pour-quoi la vie est gaie.

Can it be that we can fly to mu - sic?
Di - tes moi pour-quoi, chère ma - d'moi - sel - le,

Just be-cause, just be-cause you like me?
Est-ce que par-ce que vous m'ai - mez?

Go Tell Aunt Rhodie

American Folk Song

1. Go tell Aunt Rho - die, go tell Aunt Rho - die,

Go tell Aunt Rho - die the old gray goose is dead.

2. The one she's been saving, the one she's been saving,
   The one she's been saving to make a feather bed.

3. She died in the mill pond, she died in the mill pond,
   She died in the mill pond, standing on her head.

4. The goslings are crying, the goslings are crying,
   The goslings are crying, the old gray goose is dead.

5. The gander is weeping, the gander is weeping,
   The gander is weeping, the old gray goose is dead.

Buddies and Pals

Make melody.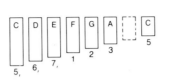

Words and music by Tom Glazer

Make harmony.

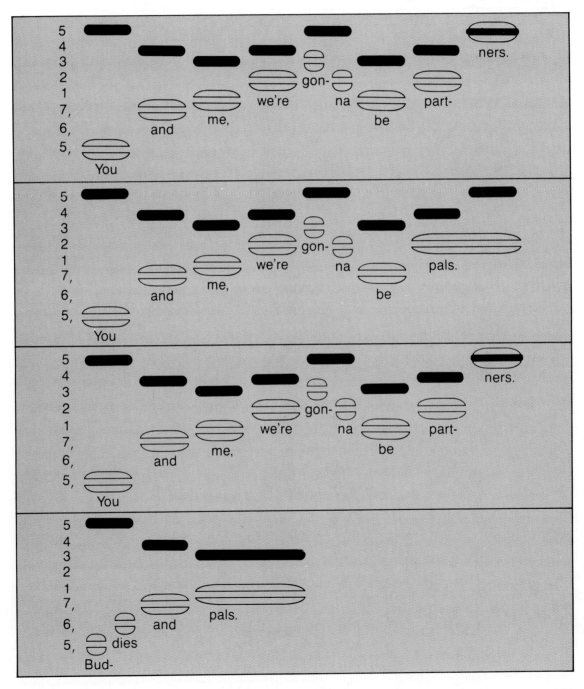

131

Who Stole the Cookie from the Cookie Jar?

Afro-American Chant

Start.

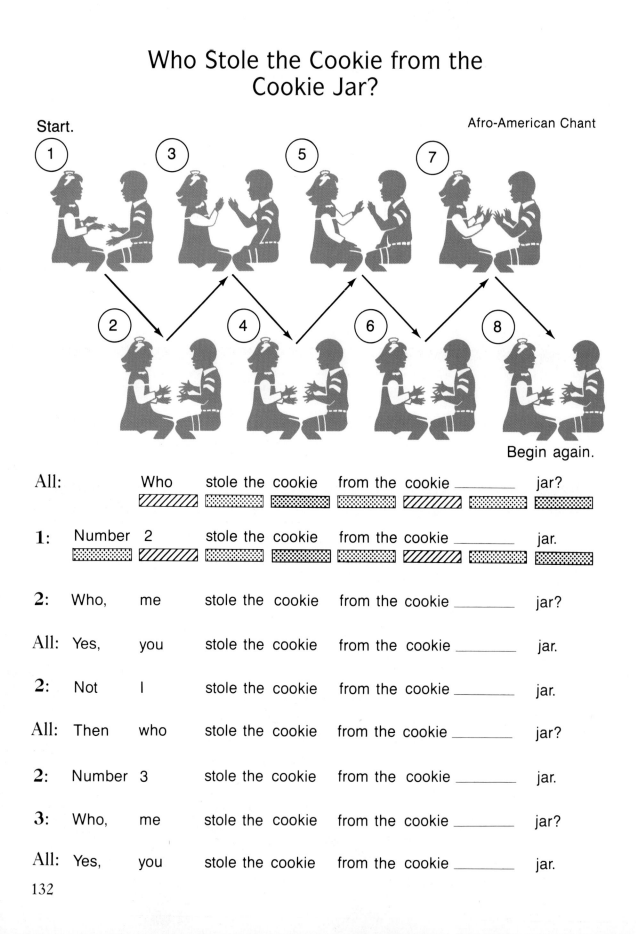

Begin again.

All:		Who	stole the	cookie	from the	cookie	_____	jar?
1:		Number 2	stole the	cookie	from the	cookie	_____	jar.
2:	Who,	me	stole the	cookie	from the	cookie	_____	jar?
All:	Yes,	you	stole the	cookie	from the	cookie	_____	jar.
2:	Not	I	stole the	cookie	from the	cookie	_____	jar.
All:	Then	who	stole the	cookie	from the	cookie	_____	jar?
2:	Number 3		stole the	cookie	from the	cookie	_____	jar.
3:	Who,	me	stole the	cookie	from the	cookie	_____	jar?
All:	Yes,	you	stole the	cookie	from the	cookie	_____	jar.

132

Place to Be

Words and music by Malvina Reynolds

1. Ev- ery- bo- dy | has a place to go,

Ev- ery- bo- dy | wants a place to be,

When birds fly, they're | swim-ming in the sky, While

fish are swim-ming in the | sea.

2. Everybody has a place to go,
   Everybody wants to be somewhere,
   Lobsters live at the bottom of the sea,
   While I'm at the bottom of the air.

133

The Cute Little Car

Words and music by Norman Cazden

Play even rhythms.

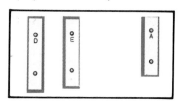

Play uneven rhythms.

What other instruments could play these rhythms?

There was a lit-tle car, __ the cut-est lit-tle car, __

The cut-est lit-tle car you ev-er did see.

And the car was on the wheels, and the wheels were on the ground,

And the en-gine in the car __ made the wheels go 'round.

Shake the Papaya Down

Calypso Song
Collected by W. S. Haynie

Sing the rhythm of the melody.
Play the shortest sounds.

Play the beat.

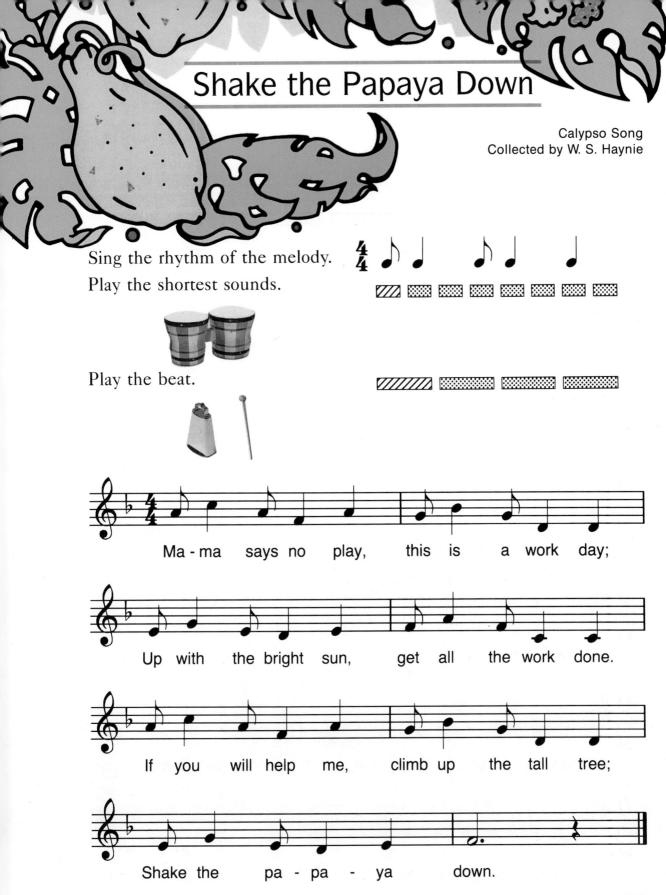

Ma - ma says no play, this is a work day;

Up with the bright sun, get all the work done.

If you will help me, climb up the tall tree;

Shake the pa - pa - ya down.

The Three Billy Goats Gruff

Words and music by Frank Luther

On a bluff,   on a bluff,
Ev-ery day,   ev-ery day,

There lived three Bil - ly Goats Gruff.
They'd run and jump _ and play.

(high voice)   *(middle voice)*
Lit - tle Bil - ly Goat, Mid - dle Bil - ly Goat,
Lit - tle Bil - ly Goat, Mid - dle Bil - ly Goat,

(heavy voice)
Great Big Bil - ly Goat Gruff.
Great Big Bil - ly Goat Gruff.

I'm a troll (foll de roll), I'm a troll (foll de roll),
I've three heads and I've three hats, I've three chins and I've three cats,

I'm a troll (foll de roll), Foll de roll de rol-ly. ___
I've six eyes and I've six ears, When I cry I cry six tears.

Trip trap, trip trap, Hop and skip, hop and skip.

I'm a troll (foll de roll), . . .

Trip trap, trip trap, Hop and skip, hop and skip,

Clip-pe-ty clop, hip-pe-ty hop, O-ver the rick-e-ty bridge. ___

Trip trap, trip trap, Hop and skip, hop and skip.

I'm a troll (foll de roll), . . .

Trip trap, trip trap, Hop and skip, hop and skip,

Clip-pe-ty clop, hip-pe-ty hop, O-ver the rick-e-ty bridge._

Trip trap, trip trap, Hop and skip, hop and skip.

I'm a troll (foll de roll), . . .

Trip trap, trip trap, Hop and skip, hop and skip,

Clip-pe-ty clop, hip-pe-ty hop, O-ver the rick-e-ty bridge._

Ev-ery day, ev-ery day, They run and jump and play,

Lit-tle Bil-ly Goat, Mid-dle Bil-ly Goat, Great Big Bil-ly Goat Gruff.

Describe Music

LISTENING

March

from *The Comedians*

by Dmitri Kabalevsky

Describe sounds
by moving,
by drawing,
with words,
with muscial pictures

■ ■ ■ ■   or   ♩ ♩ ♩

Snow-White Little Burro

Chilean Folk Melody

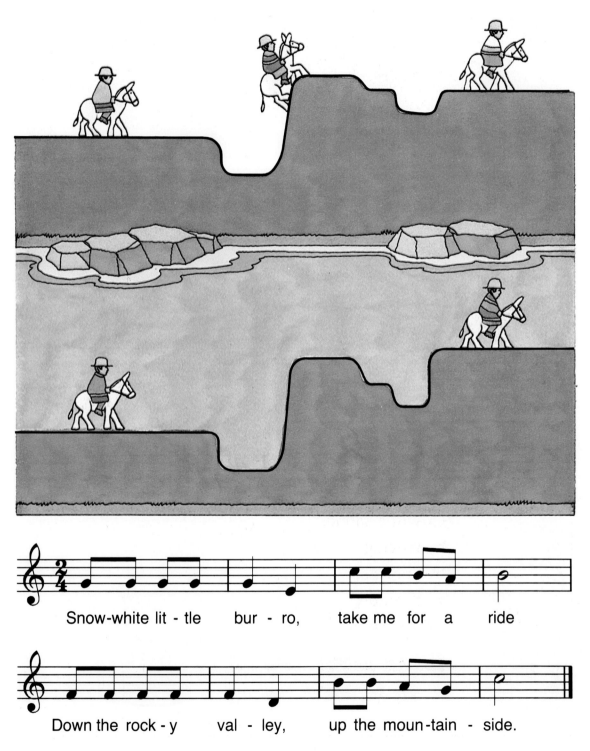

Snow-white lit - tle bur - ro, take me for a ride

Down the rock - y val - ley, up the moun-tain - side.

All Night, All Day

Spiritual

All night

All day

Refrain

All night, all _____ day,

An - gels watch-ing o - ver me, my Lord, __

All night, all _____ day,

Fine

An - gels watch-ing o - ver me. _____

Angels watching over me   Now I lay me down to sleep

Verse

1. Now   I   lay   me   down__ to   sleep,
2. If   I   die   be -   fore __ I   wake,

An - gels   watch -ing o - ver   me, my   Lord,__

Pray   the   Lord   my   soul __ to   keep,
Pray   the   Lord   my   soul __ to   take,

D.C. al Fine

An - gels   watch - ing o - ver   me. _____

A Tempo Game

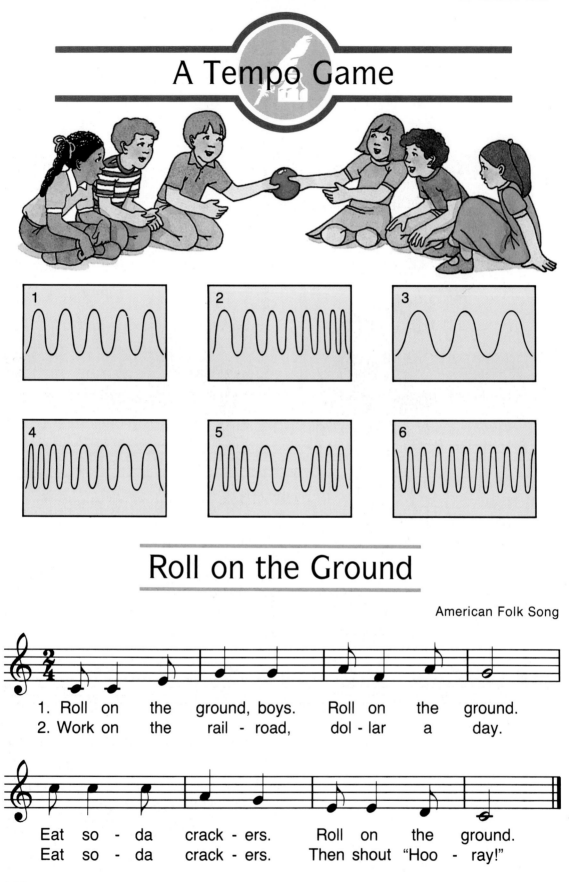

Roll on the Ground

American Folk Song

1. Roll on the ground, boys. Roll on the ground.
2. Work on the rail - road, dol - lar a day.

Eat so - da crack - ers. Roll on the ground.
Eat so - da crack - ers. Then shout "Hoo - ray!"

144

To Paree

French Folk Song

1	2	3	4
Forte	Piano	<	>

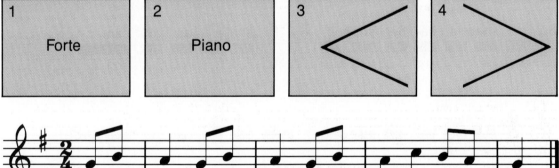

1. To Pa - ree, to Pa - ree, po-ny gray will car-ry me.

2. To Verdun, to Verdun
   On a little pony brown.

3. To Cambrai, to Cambrai
   On a little pony bay.

4. Now come back, now come back
   On a little pony black.

Going to Kentucky

Playground Game

We're go-ing to Ken-tuck-y, 𝄽 we're go-ing to the fair,

𝄽 to see a se-ño-ri-ta 𝄽 with ros-es in her hair.

So shake it, ba-by, shake it, shake it all you can.

Shake it like a milk shake, 𝄽 and drink it if you can.

So rum-ble to the bot-tom, rum-ble to the top,

Turn a-round and turn a-round un-til you make a stop!

Little Chickens

Ecuadorian Folk Song

"Pi - o, pi - o, pi - o," lit - tle chick-ens sing

When they're ver-y hun - gry or want moth-er's wing.

Go to Sleep

Louisiana French Folk Song

Go to sleep, my dear lit - tle one,
Go to sleep, Pa - pa is up - stairs.

Go to sleep, Ma - ma is be - low.
When you wake, we'll all eat some cake.

Dipidu

African Folk Song

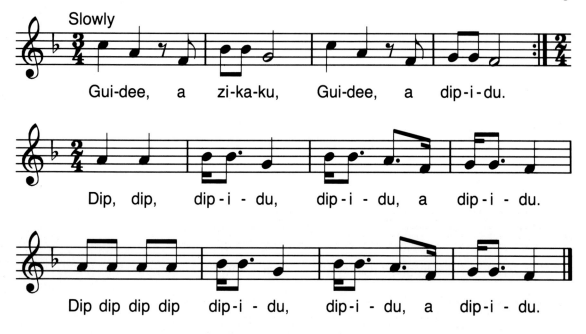

Slowly

Gui-dee, a zi-ka-ku, Gui-dee, a dip-i-du.

Dip, dip, dip-i-du, dip-i-du, a dip-i-du.

Dip dip dip dip dip-i-du, dip-i-du, a dip-i-du.

Move to music from **Mexico.**

Show the steady beat.

Show when you hear different instruments.

Move to music from **Africa.**

Choose one instrument.

Move when you hear its sound.

Move to music from **Japan.**

When will you make smooth movements?

When will you make sharp movements?

The Lotus

Japanese Folk Song

Let's o - pen, o - pen now.

Which flower shall we o - pen _ now?

Let us o - pen lo - tus _ flower,

But as soon as it is o - pen,

Quick-ly a-gain it clo - ses.

Create Music

LISTENING

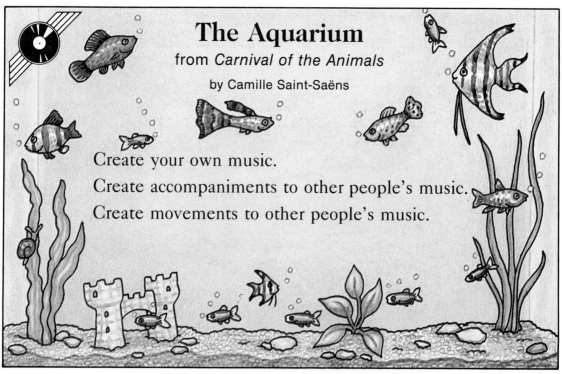

The Aquarium
from *Carnival of the Animals*

by Camille Saint-Saëns

Create your own music.

Create accompaniments to other people's music.

Create movements to other people's music.

The Cat

Words by B.A.

Music by Ronald Lo Presti

Play and sing:

p

Why-a-mese are Si - a-mese so sly - a-mese?

pp   *ff*

They sneak and creep; then sud-den-ly they leap!

Sounds

How many different sounds can you find on one instrument?

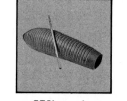

What happens if you . . .
tap it in different places?
tap it with different sound starters?
stop the sound?
let the sound die away?
put the instrument inside a box?

Choose three sounds you made.
Ask your teacher to tape the sounds.
Play the sounds on the tape recorder
at different speeds.
What happens to the sounds?

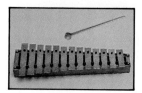

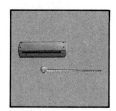

LISTENING

Brontosaurus

By Curtis Bahn and Kimiko Hahn

Listen to these sounds.

Can you imagine what instrument made them?

Can you move to the sounds?

Choose just one sound you like.

Move only when you hear it.

152

The Squirrel

Anonymous

UP

Furly Curly

HIPPITY HOP

Whisky Frisky

Whirly Twirly

DOWN

Snappity
Crackity

Whisky, frisky,
Hippity hop,
Up he goes
To the tree top!

Whirly, twirly,
Round and round,
Down he scampers
To the ground.

Furly, curly,
What a tail!
Tall as a feather,
Broad as a sail!

Where's his supper?
In the shell,
Snappity, crackity,
Out it fell.

153

March Past of the Kitchen Utensils

from *The Wasps*

by Ralph Vaughan Williams

Which parts are marching music? dancing music?

Jan Ken Pon

Japanese Folk Song

Scissors   Paper   Stone

O to-mo-da - chi,   O ha - in - na - sai,
O to-mo-da - chi,   Will you skip with me?

San yo ra shu Sa te Jan Ken Pon!
"Thank you, I will." Well, then, Jan Ken Pon!

O ma - ke no o - ka - ta wa O nu - ke - na - sai.
Ah, my friend, you lost the game and so you must be gone.

155

Lines, Colors, and Shapes

Find lines, colors, and shapes
in this painting.

Two Circles by Kandinsky, Collection, Solomon
R. Guggenheim Museum, New York. Oil and tempera
on canvas, 25 5/8 × 36 3/8″, March 1935.

Can you find lines, colors,
and shapes in the picture
on this page?

Sleeping Cat, woodcut by © Jacques Hnizdovsky,
published by Associated American Artists. 9 × 10 3/4".

The Angel Band

South Carolina Folk Song

Verse

There was one, there were two, there were three lit-tle an-gels,
There were four, there were five, there were six lit-tle an-gels,

There were seven, there were eight, there were nine lit-tle an-gels,

Ten lit - tle __ an-gels in the band. _____

Refrain

Was-n't that a band, Sun - day morn - ing,

Sun - day morn - ing, Sun - day morn - ing?

Was-n't that a band, Sun-day morn-ing, Sun-day morn-ing soon? __

Open the Gate

Someone can play this accompaniment
on the bass xylophone.

Form a line of partners
to make a gate.
Everyone chant:

O - pen the gate   as   high   as   the   sky   and

let   the   king   and   queen   pass   by.

Merry Monarch

Words and music by B.A.

1–2. Mer - ry, mer - ry maj - es - ties,   might - y may they be.

A   mar - vel - ous, mag - nan - i - mous   mon - arch is { he! / she! }

Special Times

Mama, Bake the Johnny Cake, Birthday Comin'

Words and music by
Blake Alphonso Higgs (Blind Blake)

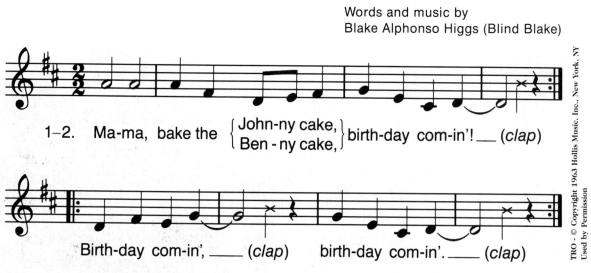

1–2.   Ma-ma, bake the { John-ny cake, / Ben - ny cake, } birth-day com-in'! ___ (*clap*)

Birth-day com-in', ___ (*clap*)   birth-day com-in'. ___ (*clap*)

America

Words by Samuel F. Smith

Music attributed to Henry Carey

1. My coun - try, 'tis of thee,
2. My na - tive coun - try, thee,

Sweet land of lib - er - ty, Of thee I sing;
Land of the no - ble free, Thy name I love;

Land where my fa - thers died, Land of the pil - grims' pride,
I love thy rocks and rills, Thy woods and tem - pled hills;

From ev - ery _ moun - tain - side Let _ free - dom ring.
My heart _ with _ rap - ture thrills Like _ that a - bove.

Who Would Ride a Broomstick?

Words by Rowena Bastin Bennett

Music by Fred Willman

Verse

1. Who would ride a broom-stick, as the witch-es do,

Straight a - cross the peb - bly stars on a street of blue?

Refrain

I should! I should! (If Moth - er came, too.)

I should! I should! (If Moth - er came, too.)

2. Who would take a wildcat, with eyes all yellow-green,
To ride upon his broomstick late on Halloween?
I should! I should! (If Mother sat between.)
I should! I should! (If Mother sat between.)

All Things Bright and Beautiful

Words by Cecil Frances Alexander

German Melody

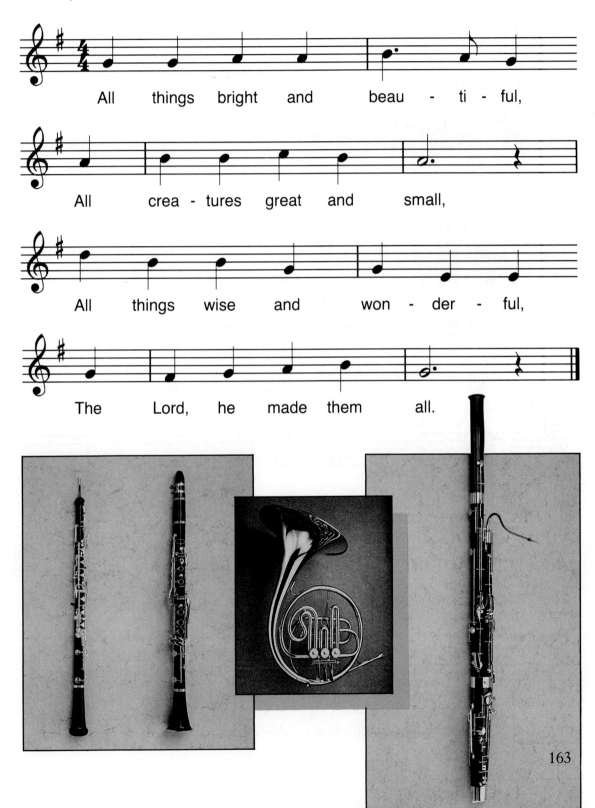

All things bright and beau - ti - ful,

All crea - tures great and small,

All things wise and won - der - ful,

The Lord, he made them all.

Over the River and through the Wood

Words by Lydia Maria Child

Traditional Tune

Crisply

1. O - ver the riv - er and through the wood,
2. O - ver the riv - er and through the wood,

To grand - fa - ther's house we go; _____
And straight through the barn - yard gate, _____

The horse knows the way to car - ry the sleigh
We seem — to go ex - treme - ly slow,

Through the white and drift - ed snow. ——
It —— is so hard to wait! ——

O - ver the riv - er and through the wood,
O - ver the riv - er and through the wood,

Oh, how the wind does blow! ——
Now grand-moth-er's cap I spy! ——

It stings the toes and bites the nose
Hur - rah for the fun! Is the pud - ding done?

As o - ver the ground we go. ——
Hur - rah for the pump - kin pie! ——

Hanukah

Jewish Folk Song

Lively

1. Ha-nu-kah,　　Ha-nu-kah,　　Fes-ti-val of　　Lights;
2. Ha-nu-kah,　　Ha-nu-kah,　　What a mer-ry　　time;

Can-dles glow　　in a row,　　Sev-en days, eight nights.
Cakes to eat,　　what a treat,　　See the fac - es　　shine!

Ha-nu-kah,　　Ha-nu-kah,　　Make your drei-dels　　spin
Ha-nu-kah,　　Ha-nu-kah,　　Sing and dance this　　way:

Round and round,　　round and round,　　Ev-ery-one join　　in!
Round and round,　　round and round,　　Hap-py hol - i - day!

Now Sing We All Merrily

Welsh Tune

1. Now sing we all merrily, Christmas is here,

The day we love best of all days in the year.

2. Bring out the green holly, the fir, and the bay,
   And deck every cottage for glad Christmas Day.

3. The children are happy, with presents in hand,
   From Santa to children all over the land.

Mary Had a Baby

Spiritual

Tenderly

1. Mar - y had a ba - by, Yes, Lord,

Mar - y had a ba - by, Yes, my Lord,

Mar - y had a ba - by, Yes, Lord,

The peo-ple keep a - com-ing and the train has gone.

2. What did Mary name him . . .   5. Born in lowly stable . . .
3. Mary named him Jesus . . .   6. Where did Mary lay him . . .
4. Where was Jesus born . . .   7. Laid him in a manger . . .

You can play an accompaniment for this song
with just two tones.

Play this pattern three times,

then play this pattern once.

168

Scatter the Bonbons

English words by B.A.

Mexican Folk Song

1. Serve up the bon-bons, sug - ar plum can-dies
1. *E - chen con - fi - tes y ca - ne - lo - nes*
2. Come, lit - tle chil-dren, come, don't de - lay now.

For all the ones who are glut - ton - ous chil-dren.
pa - ra los ni - ños que son muy tra - go - nes.
Come with your bas - ket of crun-chy good pea-nuts.

3. From little green pines
   To the tall torch pines
   Our little shoes
   Go hopping and jumping.

4. I don't want gold,
   I don't want silver,
   All that I want
   Is to break the piñata.

Bells

by B.A.

Ring! Ching! Bong! Dong!

Bells on the steeple
Or in hands of people
Ring out good tidings
and peace to all men.

Choose ringing sounds to help express this poem.

All I Want for Christmas Is My Two Front Teeth

Words and music by Don Gardner

A

All I want for Christ-mas is my two front teeth,

my two front teeth, see, my two front teeth!

Gee, if I could on - ly have my two front teeth,

then I could wish you "Mer - ry Christ - mas."

B

It seems so long since I could say

"Sis - ter Su - sie sit - ting on a this - tle!" ⌣

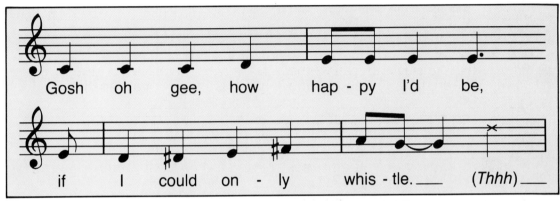

Gosh oh gee, how hap-py I'd be,

if I could on-ly whis-tle. ___ (*Thhh*) ___

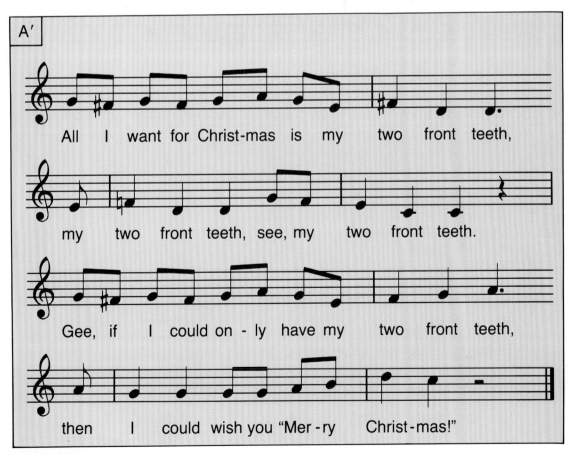

A′

All I want for Christ-mas is my two front teeth,

my two front teeth, see, my two front teeth.

Gee, if I could on-ly have my two front teeth,

then I could wish you "Mer-ry Christ-mas!"

Valentine, Valentine

Words and music by Robert D. Sittig

1–4. Val-en-tine, val-en-tine, who is my val-en-tine,

Is it you? _____

1. Mud tur-tle shells would be bet-ter than bells
2. Foam rub-ber cake would be eas-y to make
3. Flow-ers and can-dy and ev-ery-thing grand
4. Gig-gles and whis-pers and may-be a kiss

for my val - en - tine, yes,

Mud tur-tle shells would be fine. _____
Foam rub-ber cake would be fine. _____
I am your val - en - tine true. _____
I am your val - en - tine true. _____

Call to Colors
The Star-Spangled Banner

Words by Francis Scott Key

Traditional Melody

The Flag Goes By

Words by Henry Holcomb Bennett

Music by William S. Haynie

1. Hats off! Hats off! A - long the street there comes
2. Hats off! Hats off! A - long the street there comes

A blare of bu - gles, a ruf - fle of drums,
A blare of bu - gles, a ruf - fle of drums,

A flash of col - or be - neath the sky:
And loy - al hearts are ___ beat - ing high:

Hats off! Hats off! The flag is pass - ing by.
Hats off! Hats off! The flag is pass - ing by.

173

Acknowledgments

Grateful acknowledgment is made to the following copyright owners and agents for their permission to reprint the following copyrighted material. Every effort has been made to locate all copyright owners; any errors or omissions in copyright notice are inadvertent and will be corrected as they are discovered.

"All I Want for Christmas is My Two Front Teeth," words and music by Don Gardner, copyright © 1946 (Renewed) WARNER BROS. INC. All Rights Reserved. Used by Permission. Recording licensed through the Harry Fox Agency.

"All the Pretty Little Horses," reprinted and recorded by permission of the publishers, from ON THE TRAIL OF NEGRO FOLKSONGS, by Dorothy Scarborough, Cambridge, Mass.: Harvard University Press, Copyright 1925 by Harvard University Press; 1953 by Mary McDaniel Parker.

"The Angel Band," from 36 South Carolina Spirituals by C. Diton, copyright © 1957 by G. Schirmer Inc. Copyright Renewed. International Copyright Secured. All Rights Reserved. Used by permission of Music Sales Corporation for G. Schirmer Inc. Recording licensed through the Harry Fox Agency.

"Black Horse," words and music by Malvina Reynolds, copyright © 1957 Schroder Music Co. (ASCAP). All rights reserved. Reprinted and recorded by permission.

"Boa Constrictor," by Shel Silverstein. TRO—© Copyright 1962, 1968 and 1969 by Hollis Music, Inc., New York, NY. Used by Permission. Recording licensed through the Harry Fox Agency.

"Buddies and Pals," from Do Your Ears Hang Low?—50 More Musical Fingerplays, by Tom Glazer, Doubleday & Co., New York. © Songs Music, Inc., Scarborough, N.Y. 10510. By permission. Recording licensed through the Harry Fox Agency.

"Charlie Over the Ocean," from Elephant Jam by Sharon, Lois and Bram, arranged by Frank Metis. Copyright © 1980 by Pachyderm Music. Reprinted and recorded by permission of McGraw-Hill Ryerson, Ltd., Canada.

"Come Sailing With Me," originally "Come Rowing With Me," Italian folk song. Source: DISCOVERING MUSIC TOGETHER, Book 2, Teachers Edition by Charles Leonhard et al., Copyright © 1967, 1970, by Follett Educational Corporation and Allyn and Bacon, Inc.

"The Cute Little Car," words and music by Norman Cazden. TRO—© Copyright 1961 Melody Trails, Inc., New York, NY. Used by Permission. Recording licensed through the Harry Fox Agency.

"Dipidu," a South African folk song, from Loet Ons Almal Saam Sing: Songbook For Girl Guides of South Africa. Copyright © 1962, by World Around Songs. Reprinted and recorded by permission.

"DITES-MOI (Tell Me Why)," words by Oscar Hammerstein II and music by Richard Rodgers. Copyright © 1949 by Richard Rodgers and Oscar Hammerstein II. Copyright Renewed. Williamson Music Co., Owner of publication and allied rights throughout the Western Hemisphere and Japan. All Rights Administered by Chappell & Co., Inc. International Copyright Secured ALL RIGHTS RESERVED Used by Permission. Recording licensed through the Harry Fox Agency.

"Doctor Foster Went to Gloster," music by Mary Tolbert, words from Mother Goose, from This Is Music For Today, Grade 2, © Copyright, 1971, by Allyn and Bacon, Inc. Melody used by permission of the publisher.

"The Flag Goes By," music by William S. Haynie. Copyright © 1966 by Gulf Music Company. Reprinted and recorded by permission.

"The Grand Old Duke of York," by Maureen Roffey and Bernard Lodge. Reproduced by permission of The Bodley Head, London.

"H-A-double P-I-N-E-double S," words and music by Doug Nichol, copyright © 1975 by Doug Nichol. Reprinted and recorded by permission.

"Hallelu," originally "Song of Praise," a Hebrew folk song translated and adapted by Judith K. Eisenstein, copyright © 1938 and renewed copyright © 1966 by Judith K. Eisenstein. Reprinted and recorded by permission of the author.

"Hot Dog," from Singing Every Day of OUR SINGING WORLD series, © Copyright, 1959, 1957, 1949, by Silver, Burdett & Ginn, Inc. Reprinted and recorded by permission.

"If I Were a Flower," by Joseph and Nathan Segal, copyright © 1971 by Nathan Segal. Reprinted and recorded by permission of Nathan Segal.

"If You Can't Say Something Nice," by Richard M. Sherman and Robert B. Sherman. Copyright © 1963 Wonderland Music Company, Inc. Reprinted by Permission. Recording licensed through the Harry Fox Agency.

"I Live in a City," words and music by Malvina Reynolds, © 1960 Schroder Music Co. (ASCAP). Used by permission. All rights reserved.

"In the Evening Moonlight," translation of "Au Clair de la Lune," adapted from A GOLDEN SONGBOOK translated and harmonized by Katharine Tyler Wessells, © 1981 Western Publishing Company, Inc. Used by permission.

"It's All Right to Cry," by Carol Hall © 1972 Free To Be Foundation, Inc. Used by Permission of Levine and Epstein, Attorneys for Free To Be Foundation, Inc.

"I've a Pair of Fishes," a Jewish folk tune, words by J. Lilian Vandevere, from A Treasury of Jewish Folksong, selected and edited by Ruth Rubin. Copyright © 1950 by Schocken Books Inc. Renewed © 1977 by Ruth Rubin. Reprinted and recorded by permission of Schocken Books Inc.

"Join Into the Game," originally "(Come On And) JOIN INTO THE GAME," words and music by Paul Campbell. TRO—© Copyright 1951 and renewed 1979 Folkways Music Publishers, Inc., New York, NY. Used by Permission. Recording licensed through the Harry Fox Agency.

"The Lollipop Tree," words by Joe Darion, music by George Kleinsinger. Copyright © 1951 renewed © 1978 by Joe Darion and George Kleinsinger. Reproduced and recorded by permission of Alan S. Honig, C.P.A., Administrator, Alan S. Honig & Company.

"Mama Bake the Johnny Cake, Birthday Comin'," adapted from "Mama Bake the Johnny Cake,—Christmas Comin'," words and new music arrangement by Blake Alphonso Higgs (Blind Blake). TRO—© Copyright 1963 Hollis Music, Inc., New York, NY. Used by Permission. Recording licensed through the Harry Fox Agency.

"Mary Mack," melody by Ella Jenkins, first verse adapted by Ella Jenkins. Copyright © 1966 assigned to Ellbern Publishing, Chicago, Illinois. (ASCAP). Reprinted and recorded by permission.

"Michael Finnegan," from THE FIRESIDE BOOK OF CHILDREN'S SONGS, edited by Marie Winn, musical arrangements by Allan Miller. Copyright © 1966 by Marie Winn and Allan Miller. Reprinted and recorded by permission of SIMON & SCHUSTER, Inc.

Photo Credits

Art Credits

Alphabetical Index of Music

176

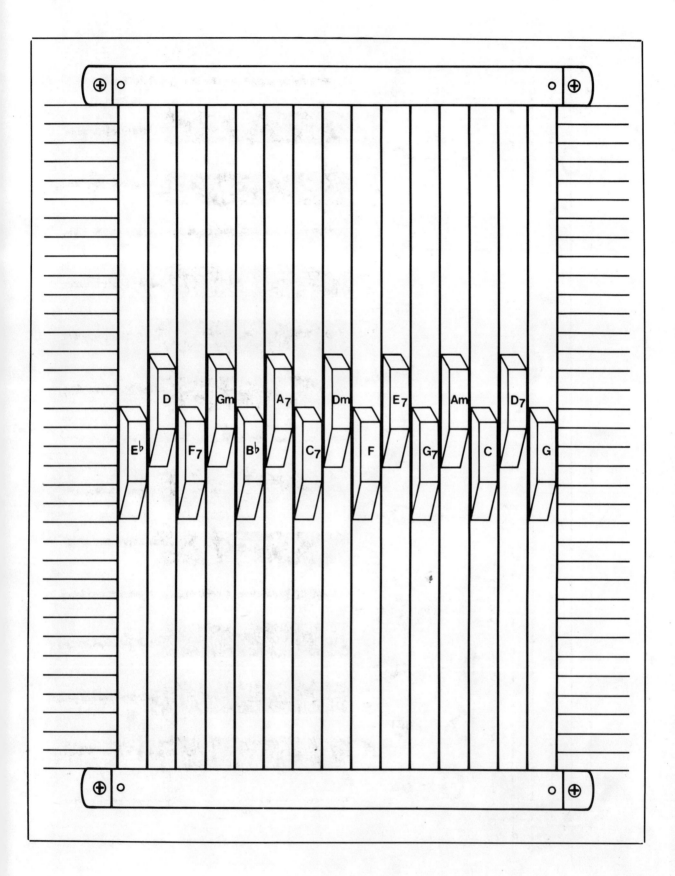